MW00911757

BOUND BY DUTY

Walking the Beat with Canada's Cops

PAT CAPPONI

VIKING
Published by the Penguin Group
Penguin Books Canada Ltd, 10 Alcorn Avenue, Toronto, Ontario, Canada M4V 3B2
Penguin Books Ltd, 27 Wrights Lane, London W8 5TZ, England
Penguin Putnam Inc., 375 Hudson Street, New York, New York 10014, U.S.A.
Penguin Books Australia Ltd, Ringwood, Victoria, Australia
Penguin Books (NZ) Ltd, cnr Rosedale and Airborne Roads, Albany, Auckland 1310, New Zealand

Penguin Books Ltd, Registered Offices: Harmondsworth, Middlesex, England

First published 2000

10 9 8 7 6 5 4 3 2 1

Printed and bound in Canada on acid-free paper ∞
Text design and typesetting by Laura Brady

CANADIAN CATALOGUING IN PUBLICATION DATA

Capponi, Pat 1949–
Bound by duty

ISBN 0-670-88931-8

1. Police – Canada. 2. Police – Canada – Attitudes. I. Title

HV8157.C36 2000 363.2'0971 C00-931040-1

Visit Penguin Canada's website at **www.penguin.ca**

Dedicated with thanks to:

Paul Quinn
Nora McCabe
Reva Gerstein
Diana Capponi
Joey Slinger
June Callwood
Cynthia Good
Ernest Hirschbach
Bev Slopen
Elizabeth Gray
Pamela Fralick
Barbara Berson
Scott Sellers
Julia Capponi
Laurie Hall
and all the folks at A-Way Express

Contents

The Proposal and the Project

"Cops. That's what your next book should be about." That's what my publisher suddenly said to me while we were discussing a recent episode of *Law and Order*. That suggestion was all it took—and that was about how much direction I was given.

My ideas soon got focused. My interest was in the men and women who have chosen policing: what motivated them and what they found out when they joined, how the nature of the job affected them, and what effects they had on the job.

I come from a segment of society that hasn't the powerful interest, or investment, in protecting private property, prohibiting illegal drugs, controlling prostitution, and "cleaning the streets" that mainstream society has. For us, the sight of a blue uniform often acts as a red flag rather than a comfort.

The people from the communities I know best—the marginalized, the poor, the addicted, the mentally ill, the homeless—know, more than most, the realities of Canadian law enforcement, its flaws, its abuses, its golden moments. These people understand what it's like to be at the mercy of others (too many others), whether they're being interrogated by a welfare worker, condemned by Children's Aid, turned away from shelters, or committed to an institution. These people know that there has always been a two-tier system of policing: one for the have's, one for the have-not's. Out on the street, in city parks and alleyways, in rundown bars, and boarding homes, you learn fast that an unhappy cop can be as lethal and destructive as a disgruntled postal worker.

As a community worker in a large drop-in centre, I knew that when I dialed 911, it wouldn't be the chief of police responding. I've seen the casual brutality of a cop's street enforcement, and I've heard attitude with a capital A, characterized by resentment, burn-out, and denigrating labels.

I also remembered meeting Bill Currie, when he chaired the Board of the Centre for Addiction and Mental Health, and when he sat as a member of the Golden Committee on Homelessness. His capacity and willingness to learn from the disenfranchised impressed me.

A police force is not a monolith; it is a living, breathing organization of individuals. I've felt the real empathy and determination of cops investigating the deaths of those labelled "mentally ill," for the coroner's office; I know officers who have a far greater understanding of the challenges facing our communities than most social workers.

When this project was offered to me, I didn't set out with an agenda. I am, by nature, curious about people and what makes them tick, and I welcomed the opportunity to explore the "closed" world of policing. To see me, in my blue jeans and cowboy hat—blaring counterculture—it would be reasonable to expect I'd have difficulty getting cops to trust me enough to talk, but that wasn't the case.

Names of potential "subjects" came up in conversations with community groups, from professionals working on national drug strategies, from civilians participating in the training of recruits, and from the police themselves—sometimes even from newspaper headlines. And if any hesitancy existed during the first phone call or meeting, it dissipated as time went on, as trust was established. Some of my subjects went out and bought my books, others researched me on the Internet. It also helped when I could recite the list of cops already talking to me, something I often resorted to, to quell suspicions.

I am more interested in people than places; this book has many Toronto police officers, which is appropriate since it's easier to see the problems of policing in a big, highly diverse city, where the politicization of the police associations and community relations have reached their nadir.

I did make an effort to speak to the St. John's, Newfoundland police chief, interested as I was in the impact of guns on a force that went without them for years, but kept being told how busy everyone was, which I had some difficulty believing. He was the only one who ducked my calls.

It would be valuable, perhaps, for another book to compare forces, and even departments; but for this book, I wanted to understand why people joined and why they stayed.

They believed I would be balanced and fair, and in most cases, that's all it took. They talked about their backgrounds; what led them to want to be police; their training; the level of acceptance or rejection they encountered from their peers; what it's like to be a woman, or a person of colour, wearing the uniform; how they see their leadership; how they view the public they are sworn to serve and protect, and how they see "the job" and its changing nature.

What I found intriguing was how little these men and women had in common before entering the force, the myriad differences in upbringing, class, education, and outlook, even in their broader life experience. They defy stereotyping.

And yet, in the end, the police will tell you: "A cop is a cop is a cop."

I was also interested in how police forces deal with difference within their ranks, and the renewed push to bring in visible minorities. Thirty years ago, admitting to being Catholic could be a career killer. Twenty-five years ago, women who joined the police were seen by their uniformed brethren as "dykes or whores"—why else would a woman want to spend all her time around men? In the last decade, officers have refused to partner with women, with blacks, with Asians; they aren't seen as real cops. The suspicions are that the standards have been lowered to accommodate a political agenda.

This is exacerbated when women or blacks are promoted. To those who fail the sergeants' exam time after time, the promotion of a member of a minority group can't possibly be on merit. But now that police forces are valuing education over physical size, competency over the number of years worked, those left behind feel under siege, and resentment rules.

I wanted to know how prepared our police forces are to de-institutionalize themselves, step away from the traditional, reactive form of policing, and move into the more proactive, and user-friendly model of community policing.

Do they carry their prejudice and attitudes into the streets with them? Will their peers call them on it if they do? In an increasingly multicultural society, can a police force, overwhelmingly composed of conservative white males, be trusted by the communities it serves? And what do those officers whose mandate includes training in diversity—exposing cops to members of the gay and lesbian communities, visible minorities, and psychiatric survivors—feel they're accomplishing?

You'll hear from those in senior ranks, who are setting the new direction, and you'll hear, too, the continuing frustration of women on the force over the police response to domestic abuse or sexual assault, and of dealing with superiors who just don't like women.

The Toronto Star carried a front-page photo of Toronto's

new police chief, Julian Fantino, hanging his favourite picture in his office—a Norman Rockwell print: everyone white, everything simple. Never mind that when that picture was painted, a man of Italian descent would never have gotten the top job.

We have those in our police departments who would like to turn back the clock, to return their former eras of privilege and status and impunity. Others are just as determined to drag the force—kicking and screaming if necessary—into the 21st century.

For me, it was like travelling to a strange city: I was looking forward to exploring its exotic newness, but I sometimes encountered structures and individuals that were all too familiar. People are people. Wherever we gather, whatever we do, we carry our basic nature with us. But so do the organizational structures that arrange and direct our days: government bureaucracies, schools, agencies, institutions—any public body with mandates and mission statements, budgets and hierarchies, clients and staff, and some form of accountability.

I have had more than a nodding acquaintance with these "city/states" over the course of my life. I've viewed their machinations from inside and out, looked at the nature of power and powerlessness as it affects all levels of staffing. I've spoken with the disaffected and tried, in some cases, to bring about change. It seems to be my peculiar destiny to have this inside-out awareness of institutions. I seem to need to understand, from top to bottom, the nature of power versus the nature and response of the individual.

I had expected the police to be different. And in some ways they are. I've met and talked with honourable men and women, who began their careers with good intentions, wanting to make a difference in their communities. You'll meet them, too, and you'll see what wears them down, that peculiar institutional alchemy that turns gold into lead, enthusiasm into bone-deep cynicism.

No agency or institution, despite public pronouncements to the contrary, embraces change. Change is equated with threat—to job security, to job satisfaction, to "the way things are done." When change is seen as politically motivated, a sop to political correctness or public pressure, it will encounter the most resistance—and resistance will slow the pace of change to a crawl.

Police forces are experiencing change in their mandates, in the move away from traditional policing to the community policing model. They are also seeing change in who gets hired, leaving the majority, all sprung from the same mould—big, white, and male—feeling devalued.

Women, people of colour, gays and lesbians, and the disabled may have a legal right to gain a position within an institution but, once in, they are left to fight their own battles against resentment and discrimination, attitudes and reprisals. I once thought that prejudice was a result of poor education, but I've encountered it often enough to realize that it permeates most institutional life. To have a world without prejudice, we'd need a world without people.

Whether it's religion, or gender, colour or ethnicity, difference is seen as a threat to the status quo. Recently, the

University of Toronto was slammed by the Ontario Human Rights Commission for denying tenure to a professor, a visible-minority person, and then punishing him for complaining. In the United States, an attempt to bring in the first Catholic Chaplain for the House of Representatives created a public furor. The treatment of women in the Canadian Army was exposed in national magazine articles as abusive and exploitative. During the lead up to the U.S. presidential elections, we heard about Bob Jones University and their ban (subsequently rescinded) on inter-racial dating. We like zero tolerance for crimes children commit, but we don't impose the same standard for adults within our public institutions.

Prejudice is endemic in our police forces; it would be surprising if it wasn't. It can serve as a lightning rod for general discontent and feelings of powerlessness.

No agency or institution welcomes outside scrutiny. Insiders feel that outsiders can't understand the nature of the work, the difficulties faced, the day-to-day realities. *Omertà*, the Mafia's code of silence, is part of institutional life, whether it's called the Blue Wall of Silence, or loyalty, or just keeping your job.

I've learned in life how afraid most people are to stand up, to stand out. I know the desperate desire for conformity we crave in high school, peaking during our work years, the need to be seen as a team player, the need to go along, to get along. That's all well and good when public pronouncements and private acts are in synch, but, all too often, silence becomes the true enemy of the people.

More than one police officer told me that if I'd seen or read about the Somalia hearings, it would give me a good grounding on how things work in the police force: poor leadership, the failure of accountability, the sacrifice of others to save oneself.

Leadership is a huge question. As police forces grow, in numbers and in militancy, so does the need for the public and the rank-and-file members to have trust and confidence in the leadership. Although the rank and file seem to generally distrust and resent those who choose the promotion track, Police Services Boards see value in hiring chiefs who've risen through the ranks, "a cops' cop" being viewed as a wonderful endorsement. However, the skill it takes to be a good cop and the skill it takes to lead a huge group of men and women would not appear to be the same.

All senior levels recognize the importance of keeping politicians at arm's length, but this distance seems to be largely illusory. Senior ranks are indistinguishable from senior government bureaucrats; police chiefs are more a hybrid of politicians and managers, even if they are frequently captured by their own mythology.

A friend of mine was walking his dog by Sunnybrook Hospital, when he saw a photographer trying to take a picture of a man on a horse. As my friend got closer, he realized the rider was Toronto's chief of police, in full ceremonial regalia, no doubt posing for his official portrait on the eve of his retirement. My friend couldn't believe how uncomfortable, how pale and uncertain and nervous the chief looked atop his mount, and decided against calling out a greeting for fear of spooking both horse and rider.

I haven't seen the finished picture yet, but I'm sure the chief will look masterly and in control. It's a good metaphor, one for our times.

I enjoyed meeting the men and women I interviewed for this book. They were under no obligation to cooperate; they could have declined or blown smoke. They chose, instead, to share both the love of their jobs and their frustrations. I make no claim to a representative selection: There are more women and minorities here than are commonly found in police forces. However, these people are the real barometers of change. I chose their voices over those of organized community activists, in the hope that cops reading this might pay more attention to their own than to those people who some police feel simply hate all cops on principle. And I wanted cops to tell their own stories, because of my own fatigue with polarization and ideology, finger-pointing and mutual accusations. Community wars always seem easier than constructive peace.

So, here's a look at the women and men who fill those intimidating uniforms. Perhaps you'll never look at a cop the same way again.

The Profession
A Cop Is a Cop Is a Cop?

STARTING THE JOB
"Not all of us are thoroughbreds"

(Throughout this chapter, you will get to know a variety of police doing diverse tasks. If you're like me, you will be struck by how different these cops are from one another, how little they have in common. I didn't deliberately set out to emphasize these differences through the selection process; they arose naturally, as names came up, as interviews were done. How did these differences affect their careers? How have their careers affected them as individuals? And how do they affect the public they are sworn to serve and protect? In a later chapter, Profiles, you'll discover more about each of their backgrounds and why they joined up.)

After graduation, new constables' first exposure to real policing comes with their training officers, and many cops remember that officer the way some of us remember our first love.

John Irwin, now a Toronto sergeant, was a bit of a hotdog starting out. He now seems reflective, a bit of an outsider.

"My partner and I were passing First Canadian Place, and I saw all these cars parked where they weren't supposed to be. It was a prohibited zone, a rush-hour route. My partner didn't want to ticket them, and I remembered being told in college that some 'old guys won't want the hassle of going along with you.' So I wrote out all these tickets, and he let me do it. Later, there was a church at Bloor and Avenue Road that had cars parked in wrong places, so I ticketed them too."

Only after emptying his ticket book did it occur to him that it was Sunday, and there were no rush-hour restrictions. He looked to his partner in panic.

"He told me that all I could do was go back and gather up all the tickets. For those cars that had already left the scene, I had to track them through their licences, apologize to them, and collect the tickets. And then the church's minister brought all the tickets, which his congregation got, down to the station."

And then there was the chase, also in his first few months.

"We answered this call at the St. George subway station, and I'm hot-dogging it, jumping over the turnstile, racing down the stairs. I figured I'd left the 'old guy' in the dust, but when I got to the platform and turned around, he's right behind me. No better way to keep a check on a young cop's ego. He was an excellent training officer."

Ken Higgins, now Vancouver's deputy chief, also remembers early patrols in that city's Downtown Eastside (DES), with his "trainer."

A report of a stabbing in a pub came over the air, and the cop with Ken immediately started walking towards a different pub, went right to the back, and arrested the culprit. That cop knew his community, and it was a lifelong lesson for Ken.

Karen Bell is now a sergeant with the Anishinabek Police Services. Her first coach officer weighed about three hundred pounds. Walking down the street with him, people tended to move out of the way.

"We went to Bloor and Bathurst, he shuts off the traffic lights and sticks me in the middle of the street: 'Do the job.' I was really scared, but I pulled it off. He was really good. He took me under the Gardiner Expressway, to show me all the guys (mostly native) living there, amid thousands and thousands of empty wine bottles." Karen learned that in the morning they'd get up and wander over to some of the soup kitchens.

"I felt for them so much. For many, by this point, there's no going back. They're too ashamed of what they've done with their lives to go back home."

Margo Boyd, now a Toronto inspector, says, "Not all of us are thoroughbreds." Her training officer was a plodder and not a fan of female police.

As a group, new constables are ready to admire and emulate older cops, and if the right leadership was in place, along with healthy attitudes towards the job, it could make all the difference in the world to the public.

Toronto's deputy chief Bob Kerr sees that and more. "You can take the ideal recruit, who's had all the training, is prejudice-free, and you stick him in a squad car for eight or ten hours a day with an older cop with bad attitudes, and that ideal recruit won't stay that way for long."

RCMP Constable Jeff McArthur's first assignment was in the Surrey Detachment, in British Columbia. "This is what I'd been waiting for quite a while. Thirty minutes into my first shift, riding with my trainer, we arrested a prostitute on an outstanding warrant. It was good to be in the middle of things."

He was a little set back by "how harshly, or abruptly, our members treated the rounders [career criminals] on the beat. I don't mean physical abuse, but I was so new, I had a lot of compassion and sensitivity, and I was naïve. I wanted to believe people."

Jeff found that though his training was helpful, his real education came from day-to-day interaction with street people or responding to domestic disputes.

"If you have the patience, you can really learn from the

people themselves. I listened to this heroin addict, a really disgusting human being, he was murdered a while back, describe life on the street, pimping, selling."

Learning cannot stop at graduation. Lessons on the street can make or break a cop. But there are other lessons, about the people you work with, about the system you work within. The harshest of these lessons is that some cops are more equal than others.

FITTING IN

"So, you want to be a Dickless Tracey"

The pressure and the need to fit in is probably the strongest force acting on the individual officer. Fitting in can mean looking like everyone else. But this is harder for women and visible minorities than for white men who might feel the need to hide their differences—in intellect, in ambition, in their approach to the job—but who have the benefit of protective camouflage.

Fitting in can also mean laughing at the same jokes, no matter how personally offensive someone might find them, displaying the same level of cynicism towards the public and the media and politicians; it also requires an uncritical acceptance of how things are done, how the police really operate on the streets.

When Bill Currie, then an OPP constable, transferred from Oak Ridges to the Snelgrove detachment in Caledon, he brought with him his reputation as a high flyer, someone who was working too hard. At his first meeting with his shift, he was told that he could lay no more than thirty charges a month. The squad had had a comfortable level of activity, and they didn't want to see that increased. Bill went out that first day and laid a lot of charges, perhaps as many as fifteen; when he returned to the squad room he set up the forms all over his desk, a very obvious rejection of the way things were done.

He felt they had a right to expect him to behave in a way that fit on a personal level, but that was, for him, very different from how he performed on the job. He knew that his corporal, who had also transferred over from Oak Ridges, would support him; which prompts the question of what he would have done if he hadn't that assurance.

Bill was older than the others; he had broader life experience and a wider range of skills. Because of this, even before he'd attended his first day of training—as a new recruit—at the old facilities on Toronto's Sherbourne Street, he'd instinctively known that the wisest course for him was to concentrate, for five years, on not standing out from his peers, to win acceptance by fitting in.

He remembers there were six women in his training class. Only one is still active on the force. Of the men, half are still working cops. As a former teacher and a principal, he was used to working with women and didn't find it particularly odd that they would want to be cops. He remembers that some of the women were the best performers in the class.

None of the detachments at that time had separate

facilities for women. It's as if the powers-that-be hope that society will finally come to its senses and revert to an all-male force, and fear that the small efforts to create a separate space will incur the resentment of male peers.

Christine Silverberg, now Calgary's police chief, and Susan McCoy, a Toronto sergeant, both entered their training with an innocence that was soon shattered.

Susan McCoy says: "It was definitely a strange environment. To my dad, there was nothing better than his daughter, and I'd been brought up to believe I could be anything I wanted; no restrictions, no limits."

For Christine: "It wasn't until I joined the police, my first job was with the Mississauga force, that I realized women were not expected to do certain things."

After completing her application, Toronto Inspector Margo Boyd was scheduled for a home interview. "I was living in a bachelor apartment on Yonge, and when the doorbell rang I was talking on the telephone, and I went 'Oh, no!' because I hadn't washed the dishes and I thought: I'll never get the job now. It was a uniformed sergeant, and we sat at my tiny kitchen table, and he said to me, 'So tell me why you want to be a Dickless Tracey.'"

She took no offense, they had a nice conversation, and she was hired.

But all these women learned pretty quickly that the majority assumption was they were either lesbians or whores—why else would they want to be around men all the time?

Susan McCoy, whose class of 121 recruits had all of three women, still bristles when she remembers being singled out as a new recruit by the drill sergeant. “We were on parade; I was the only woman there at that moment. He told me to take a step forward. I did, wondering what the hell I’d done. He ordered me to turn and face the others, and I thought, I must have really screwed up bad. He had a bit of an upper-class British accent, and when he told me to get back in line, he added, ‘I just wanted a better view of your ass.’ God help that guy if he tried to do that now.”

There was no such thing as modified training. The women competed at the same level as the men. At five foot, four inches, Margo wondered about that. “Why are you teaching me to flip someone over my shoulder? I’m not going to be doing a lot of that.”

In 1974, Christine Silverberg started her training at Aylmer, Ontario, where they housed the men in barracks. Since the women were few, only two others in her class at the time, they were placed in the former nurses’ quarters. At the time, male recruits had six weeks of training, six weeks in the field, then six more weeks of study. Because of issues around accommodation, the women had to do all the twelve weeks at the college at one go.

“I wasn’t conscious of difference at Aylmer, I probably just assumed that’s how things are. Some recruits assumed, and actually said, that I must be a lesbian or a whore. Since I was neither, even hearing that didn’t affect me.” No female solidarity there. Lesbians could fend for themselves, it seems.

They asked for volunteers for the precision drill team, but when Christine stepped forward, she was initially turned down. The instructor said that the cadence of her step would be problematic. She persisted and became a member.

Margo Boyd was accepted at a time of a big hiring push in Toronto, caused by the decision to go with "two-man cars, I mean two-person cars. For the first time, ten women had been hired together, but [once again] there were no proper facilities to handle all of us at Aylmer, so we went five and five. When I arrived, there was a huge class of 150 officers, including my group of five and three more women from the OPP and Halton Region. We stayed two to a room in the same place the instructors bunked, while the male recruits lived in dorms."

Having completed the exact same training as the men, these women were not permitted to assume the same duties. Christine wasn't issued a gun. Women were neither permitted or expected to carry weapons. Women were also not allowed to go straight into uniform. Christine was sent to work at Youth and Child investigation, sometimes getting to work undercover with the detective office and the intelligence bureau.

She remembers the issue of health benefits, which the men received, but the women were denied. When she asked about it, she was told that the city provided only for men who have to raise families, that kind of thing. "When I said that my husband was in graduate school, they answered that it wasn't their responsibility what my husband did.

I don't remember being angry so much as astonished at the lack of fairness."

Margo recalls that in 1975 females graduates were sent either to 55 or 52 Division, not for any better reason than that's where they had changing facilities for women. Susan remembers being surprised at the attitudes of the wives of the constables. "I remember my first Christmas dance, being shocked at their insecurity. They could hardly bear that their husbands would spend so many hours in a car, alone with another woman."

Margo, at 55 Division, recalls the four women in her platoon, "all raw and anxious and smart. Fifty-five Division is a really, really busy place, and we wanted to be in the busy cars. There we were in our skirts and White Cross shoes, and we carried a snub-nose five-shot in a purse. We'd be tearing around, answering fight calls, gun calls, flying on the job, always being happy. Women had to work with other women in the cars, because the wives of officers didn't want their husbands in a car with a woman at 3 a.m. If only they knew that they were probably the only ones who found their husbands lovable. But with women partnering, it was like a pajama party. We liked it so much.

"I remember being called to a fight outside the Shamrock Hotel—it used to be at Coxwell and Gerrard—we were working the midnight shift, and we roared up with flashers; another car's already at the scene, and there I go in my skirt, diving in and rolling around, grabbing and yanking guys back, cuffing them and throwing them into the back of the car. You feel a little invincible."

Susan was having a different experience. "You learn very quickly not to show emotion. I remember my partner and I responding to a call. There was a beautiful child, just over a year old, just learning to walk; it was November, and near zero, and her mother, who turned out to be mentally challenged, had her child out on the back porch wearing only a diaper and undershirt. I went to the child and she just grabbed onto my leg, snuggling, and wouldn't let go. She had a cold; her nose was running; she was probably hungry. The mother didn't understand what was wrong. I tried to explain that it was too cold for her child to be out; we had to call CAS, and the child was taken into care, but you start wondering what that poor child's future will be. When I got into the patrol car, I just started crying. My partner, who was male, looked at me with something like horror. 'What are you doing?'

"'I'm crying!'

"'You can't cry!'

"'Why not?'

"'We're supposed to be in control here!'"

Susan coped by becoming a workaholic, and by over-indulging in drinking, a practice that was very acceptable among her male peers.

"There's a lot of alcohol abuse among female officers, though they hide it better than men. Women drunks are seen as disgusting and sloppy, much worse than their male counterparts." Susan remembers doing very stupid things, like telling men she could out-drink them and at times succeeding.

Christine Silverberg was learning about her work

environment, too. "I can remember hitchhiking—although I wasn't supposed to actually get in anyone's car—with my male backup hiding in the bushes behind me. Several university-aged girls had been murdered and left in remote places, after being picked up hitchhiking along the highway. The men who would stop and ask me to get in would themselves be stopped and searched further down the road. We were looking for a match of the twine used to tie them up. I was lectured by a male teacher, cursed out by some guys who'd call me a 'fucking tramp.' That really offended the backup team. I was never scared, at least not till one of the senior detectives showed me—in an act of bravado—his unauthorized magnum. That scared me."

Christine often wasn't given the tools she needed to do the job: the big picture and how one operation fitted into it. That was not the way the men were treated, and she was sure it was a set-up for failure.

"At the time, off-track betting was illegal. I was told: Go into the place and remember everything you see. They didn't specify anything in particular, so when I came back out I wrote exactly what they'd asked for—everything: what was on the walls, what the guys were saying to each other. I'm sure 90 percent of it was totally irrelevant, but it surprised them enormously."

These women endured what they encountered without expecting the brass to ride to their rescue; there were no official complaints filed, no reprimands. They had to cope as individuals with harassment and resentments, which could make or break them. In that at least, they "fitted in."

What these women encountered is not specific to police forces, not caused simply by the nature of the job. Whatever excuses the men on the force might parade to justify their resentments, those resentments are evident in any institution coping, or failing to cope, with change. Witness what happened to the highly educated women at MIT:

> All the women who crowded into Robert Birgeneau's office five years ago [1995] remember the meeting as if it was yesterday. They recall their nervous walk across a courtyard to his office, telling jokes to ease the tension; the clunk of his big, black office door; the photo of the seven most powerful men at the Massachusetts Institute of Technology—including Birgeneau, dean of the school of science—staring them in the face.
>
> The women, all tenured science faculty, sat around the conference table with Birgeneau at the head, one by one telling of the struggles, insults, even humiliation they'd experienced during their many years at MIT. . . .
>
> Birgeneau said he knew the women who came to him were unhappy, and "had I summed up all the individual experiences myself in the past I would have realized it. If one person comes into your office and expresses some unhappiness, what you do naturally, whether that faculty member is male or female, is to explain the unhappiness based on some idiosyncrasy. . . . Here, it was not one or two people

in front of me, but 15. Hearing it all at once, it was absolutely clear the problem couldn't be explained away based on idiosyncrasy. There really was a systemic problem."

It might seem impossible that anyone who had made it to the top, to the prestigious and world-renowned MIT, could have suffered discrimination.

"These women are in the top 100th of 1 percent in their fields," Birgeneau said. "But even though they had achieved a lot scientifically, and even though they had started out so excited about their careers, twenty years later they just felt something was fundamentally wrong."

It was. Birgeneau said one woman described it as "death by a thousand pinpricks. . . ." [He] has been asked why he and MIT have had so much attention, when other institutions dealt with gender discrimination years ago.

"That is a misunderstanding," he said. In the United States and Canada there was civil rights legislation that guaranteed women rights. But what [the women] experienced was that it's one thing to legislate equality—it's another thing for women in the workplace to be treated as equals. Of course, it wasn't gross discrimination, but what these women came to understand was that part of their marginalization was a series of minor insults. ("The Science of Listening," by Kristin Rushowy, *The Toronto Star*, 3 January 2000, p. A7.)

Bill Currie, OPP deputy commissioner, tells me that complaints—about harassment and discrimination—are just now starting to come across his desk, as women are beginning to show confidence in the processes. The first "fully operative" female OPP officer was hired in 1974. Toronto's first police women were hired in 1913.

Decades later, female officers still have to struggle. The rate of change is unacceptable. Every new visible-minority officer hired has to fight the same fight, battle the same ignorance, in isolation and shame. When someone stands up, in the army, in business, and exposes how women and/or minorities are treated by their co-workers and bosses, we are often surprised. We wonder what took them so long. What we understand is the myriad pressures to silence their complaints, the self-blame, made even stronger by the senior levels, assumption that it's the individual's experience alone, and therefore the fault of that same individual.

PREJUDICE
"They never said that about Italians"

For Glen Bannen, who became a policeman in 1980, being a cop was initially like being "a wide-eyed kid in a candy store. It was a whole new experience, a whole new career. But I also found out pretty quickly—at the age of twenty-two—who my real friends were; it was painful and interesting, a unique situation to be in. At the time, some people would say: the man, the Bull, the brown man in a white man's uniform."

The situation was made even more difficult by his supervisors. "I was told pretty quickly, your job is to pinch Indians." A large part of his day was supposed to involve stopping everyone coming onto or leaving the reserve to check whether they had a licence and insurance. To Glen, it felt like harassment.

"The chief lived next door to me. I knew he didn't drink. I knew he'd had all his vehicles insured, and that he and his sons all had driver's licences. It would have been pointless to stop him. It interferes with the rights of citizens to walk freely or drive in the community without harassment. This led to major conflicts with my supervisors, and I was labelled a 'problem child.' Now it's different to stop someone who isn't wearing their seat-belt, at the same time you can check whether their licence is valid. It seemed sensible to me to first explain what the rules, what the expectations of the province, are in terms of drivers. If I stop someone for the third time, they'll say, give me the paper [the ticket] because they know what's right."

The chief was a Montreal Canadiens' fan, while Glen was a booster of the Maple Leafs. The two teams would face off maybe six times over the course of a winter, and Glen would go over to his house and talk about the game and the community, and whatever else might come up.

"I'd be told by my supervisors: 'How dare you sit and gab with the chief for an hour?!' They didn't understand the value of sharing a cup of tea with an elder, the real value of talking to people. It's funny, now twenty years later, it's all you hear as the thrust and focus of most police forces. Indians have been doing that for 10,000 years, respecting people, listening, making decisions collectively."

Glen's experience of losing old friends because of his career choice is a fairly common one. What is less common is a woman's experience of being caught between a rock and a hard place: as a woman, as a visible minority, experiencing prejudice and attitudes from the force that you defend to your peers as a place to be.

Christine Silverberg sent me a copy of her profile on CBC's *Life and Times*, on which a colleague tells the story of when, as a sergeant, she attended a training course in Ottawa, the only woman in a class of hard-bitten male sergeants. Although they never told her to her face, she became aware that they had a nickname for her—"Silvertits." On the last day of her course, as she was completing her presentation to the class (all this is on amateur videotape) she breaks off, starts unbuttoning her blouse, immediately awakening her male counterparts, moving to undo the buttons on her sleeves, a slow strip routine as she informs them she's heard their nickname for her, finally revealing, dramatically, a black camisole on which is sewn, in strips of silver fabric, SILVERTITS. A lot of laughter and applause and the Holy Grail of acceptance. She'd proved she could take it; she could give it. But it was on their terms.

When Jay Hope graduated into the ranks, he'd been

asked whether he was willing to transfer anywhere in Ontario, with special emphasis on the north. Not thinking he'd actually be sent there, but trying to be agreeable, he said sure, and mentioned his brother worked out there, teaching at a "fly-in" reserve. Jay is tall and fit, a spit-and-polish guy.

He found himself in a remote northern community of 500 people called Emo. Although he was the only black guy in town, and little kids would touch his hands to see if the colour would come out, he was accepted and treated very well. He also had some policing responsibility for four reserves in the area.

One time he was called out with other members of the force to deal with a guy who was riding a tractor into houses on one of the reserves. The guy had plowed into his third house by the time the cops arrived, and refused to climb down, aiming the tractor at yet another building. The police, including Jay, fired at him after warnings, and the fellow was wounded. None of the officers knew which bullet had connected with the guy till after forensic tests, and Jay was relieved it wasn't his shot. The day after the incident, painted in big letters on the side of a barn: "The Nigger Pulled the Trigger." Jay had a lot of trouble with that.

"I didn't get it, I mean they're closer to me than to the whites."

Karen Bell, who joined Metro Toronto police in 1989, stayed with them for nineteen months.

"I wanted either 14 or 51 Division; they were the busiest, wildest areas to work. I got 14, in the west end of Toronto, covering some of the toughest areas of town." Karen is compact and muscular, willing to mix it up in hockey and boxing.

There were a lot of derelicts in the division, many of whom were aboriginal people. She'd hear comments over the radio while she sat in her squad car, derisive and contemptuous comments about drunken Indians.

"They never said that about Italians. There was an old CIBC bank at the corner of Queen and Bathurst, and a large native group had taken to hanging out on the stairs. They would poke a hole in a can of Lysol, and breathe it in. If we had to sent a car to 'male collapsed,' everyone knew it would be a native, and cops would take their time responding."

Two police officers accused of dumping a man outside Saskatoon last January should have been charged with attempted murder, says Saskatchewan's main aboriginal group.

> [The two officers] who have been suspended without pay, were charged Tuesday (with unlawful confinement and assault) following an investigation by an RCMP task force. . . .
>
> The task force is also looking into the mysterious deaths of Rodney Naistus, 25, and Lawrence Wegner, 30. Their frozen bodies were found on January 29 and February 3 in the same area where Mr. Night

> alleges he was dumped. It is also reviewing the 1990 death of Neil Stonechild, who was found dead from exposure in Saskatoon's north industrial area, and the deaths of [three others]. The decision to charge the two officers has hit other members of the city's police force hard, said Constable Al Stickney, spokesperson for the Saskatoon Police Association. Stickney said it's important to understand that the [two officers] aren't charged in or linked to any deaths. (By Julian Branch, *The Toronto Star*, 13 April 2000, p. A9.)

Karen went to her supervisor, quietly, without registering an official complaint, told him what she kept hearing, how she felt that, as an aboriginal herself, she could not trust these officers, and requested a transfer out of the offending platoon.

She didn't just walk away, because she's not a quitter, and because "I knew people I worked with who weren't racist, and I also knew that anyone who was racist against aboriginal people would also be prejudiced against other minority groups."

Her new platoon, still with 14 Division, had eleven women out of twenty-five officers. They were all around the same age, and most were fairly inexperienced. She was still the only native but, "You know, you look for people who are minorities, too, and I was happy to see two black guys and one black woman."

Feminists would probably despair that she didn't see the

rest of the women as a "situational minority" along with the "vizmins."

Karen says that prior to her stint in 14 Division, she had no prejudices to speak of. After a year on the front lines, "I had deep-rooted ideas about a certain type of person. I couldn't believe the things that would come into my mind about blacks. I imagine Toronto has ongoing problems with this. You take a green kid, maybe twenty-one years old, your thinking becomes very distorted. Even for me, who didn't exactly come from a pristine world."

Unlike the cop slurs over the squad-car radio, "I'm a minority. I never verbalized my thoughts. It's day-in, day-out dealing only with negatives. We have to be constantly reminded that productive people come out of all the races. You really need to bring in people from different communities to talk, to help police keep a balanced attitude." After about eighteen months, Karen left 14 Division—with a mixture of regret and excitement—for a new position as constable with the OPP, who were still running Police Services at her Garden River reserve.

"I wanted to be home, and I wanted to continue my career in policing."

Except for short visits, she'd been away for eleven years. It was always home, in a way that Ottawa and Toronto could never be. But it was an uneasy homecoming—this time simply due to her gender.

"It took me about six months to win acceptance. In most native communities, men dominate everything. There was a lot of testing to see how far I could be pushed. Not being as physically strong as the male officers, it's more mentally demanding. Women have to use their mouths a hell of a lot more, their gift with the English language. I recall stopping a car on a back road, about 3:30 in the morning, five drunk men and I knew all of them. The driver didn't want to exit the car; there was a lot of verbal abuse, like 'You think you're so fucking good, no one likes you.' I had to call for backup and bust his window to get him out."

When Jay Hope first applied for permission to compete for promotion, his supervising sergeant said he couldn't, although he'd put in the minimum time necessary. In the writing of this book, I've learned enough about police to know that making waves is never appreciated: The consequences can follow you throughout your career. But the consequences didn't matter so much to Jay; what the sergeant had done by refusing what Jay was entitled to was wrong. So Jay appealed to the deputy commander and was asked to provide oral arguments to back his case.

"I knew I was home free then, the sergeant wasn't very bright."

The sergeant's decision was overturned, and he was permitted to write the exam. As they left the room together, the sergeant turned to him and said, with very deliberate wording: "All I did was call a spade a spade."

I asked Jay what prompted him to appeal his supervisor's decision—he was the first cop I'd talked to who'd gone over the head of his sergeant, he didn't just take it. My assumption was that it would be something of a career killer, so why would he risk it? Like Christine, it was the unfairness that rankled. He simply wouldn't put up with it. Much later, in 1992, several grades in rank higher, Jay wanted to give back to his community, to help heal the rift that was so obvious in Toronto between the cops and blacks.

"Five of us got together, we were looking at organizations like the Shriners, Kiwanis, and the Masons. We formed the Association of Black Law Enforcers, ABLE, to help build bridges between the black community and the Toronto police, to be mentors, and to provide programs for drug and crime awareness. Some current officers are skeptical. They don't want to stand out or do anything that could hurt their career. We tell them it's not political, not a union, and that we're working to get the chiefs on side.

"When I asked Metro how many black officers they had, they told me between 145 and 200, so it's probably closer to 145. There may be 50 in the OPP. We've just given $6,000 worth of scholarships at ABLE's annual dinner, and we had 700 attendees. But we have a long, long way to go. Race relations are not going to improve of their own accord. Police agencies have made progress in terms of policies, but you can't control what people think."

Fear that joining a service club could be negatively interpreted, and could negatively impact one's career, shows that policies are no guarantee against prejudice or reprisals.

Margo Boyd says she always wanted to fit in, even though most times she was the only woman in the room.

She wanted to be accepted as one of the guys. If they were learning how to deal with rape scenarios, she refused to be made the victim, she wanted to play the person who solved the crime. She remembers as a sergeant—and the only female—taking a six-week course, where there was lots of camaraderie, and a deputy chief handed out diplomas at the end, shaking everyone's hand but kissing her on the cheek. She was really sad that he'd done that.

DEALING WITH DANGER
"This is as good as it gets"

Jeff McArthur, now an RCMP constable, articulates well what young cops are in the job for. His detachment in Surrey was an oddball bunch, the newly minted, very ambitious go-getters like himself, fighting over who got to respond to calls—and the cagey, older, experienced officers who provided perspective, told veterans' stories, and helped the kids keep their heads. There was always something exciting going on, and if there wasn't, Jeff worked out his own way to bring it on.

"I'd go to Tim Horton's, get a big coffee to go, and nine times out of ten something would happen and the coffee would go flying out the window."

Their detachment was involved in a lot of pursuits.

"Sometimes, coming on shift, our parking lot would look like a graveyard, all the remnants of cars, up to ten sometimes, which had been in pursuits the night before. I remember one particular night when I was in the burglary section, I spotted a stolen white van, and I'd reason to believe it was full of stolen goods. The way we'd do it was to take them down by boxing them in at an intersection. Well, we do that, but the driver of the van starts ramming the squad cars back and forth, back and forth, till he has enough of an opening, and he takes off. I was in an unmarked car at the time, and unmarked cars aren't allowed to do pursuits, so we were following a ways behind, listening to the guys on the radio, watching the racing patrol cars, just in case there'd be a foot chase. I had a gut feeling he'd do a U-turn, and he did, right over the median. We knew we could get in front of him now, and he was coming at us at quite a clip, he nailed the front of my car, nailed my partner's car, and then got around me into this big, wide alley. So I've got one side of the van, my partner's on the other, we've got him bracketed, racing down the alley, the driver's cranking the steering wheel left and right, bashing me, bashing my partner, we're bouncing off the buildings. When the alley ends, he turns right and we nail him in the rear end. I was pretty much in my glory."

On night patrol, he's not sure he felt responsible for the public, or "anything grandiose or melodramatic like that. I felt more like a predator, looking suspiciously at everyone, trying to come up with a bad guy."

I felt bad for Jeff when I interviewed him from his post in Stewart (population 500), British Columbia. I could feel him chomping at the bit, as he told about his time in Surrey. There aren't many bad guys for him to catch where he is. He spends much of his time in his 80,000-square-kilometres patrol area, helping to bomb potential avalanche sites, dealing with the occasional plane or bus crash, coordinating search and rescue of lost hikers and mushroom pickers, and relocating black bears, sometimes by himself.

It's not the local dump that attracts them; that has an electric fence.

"We have streams near town where salmon spawn; there are fruit trees in town; and people aren't as careful with their garbage as they should be."

The bear trap he uses can be towed behind his car, but once they arrive at a less-civilized location, he needs to open the latch to let the bear out.

"It's a bit tricky when you're on your own."

Both he and the bear tend to run like hell once the trap is sprung, he to his car, the bear to the wide open spaces. He had an opportunity to get intimately acquainted with that trap, which is constructed like a culvert, with a grill welded onto one end and a trap door on the other, triggered by a food bag.

"We'd had a number of calls about a grizzly tearing up a lady's property, so we went out with a conservation officer—they're based about two and a half hours from here, so they're not always on hand—and a trap. Unfortunately, the grizzly was pretty smart. He'd grab a lot of the bait but never touch the food bag itself, and he went on being destructive. The guys and I went back, and they'd brought so much crap—dead beaver carcasses, rotting this and that—we thought: There is no way the bear can ignore it. As it happens, the grizzly seemed to have left town of his own accord, and I got this frantic call from the lady, pretty much begging me to get the trap out of her yard. It was apparently stinking the place out. I drove up, thinking I'd take the trap down to the dump and clean it up. You wouldn't believe the smell. So I hooked it up to the back of my car, and when I got to the dump, I had to go inside it to scoop out the crap. There were maggots and all kinds of beetles crawling all over the festering meat and carcasses. We'd had a new spring put on the trap door, thinking maybe it didn't close fast or hard enough to capture our bear, and so, just for insurance, I put a spike in the way of its closing on me.

"I'm working away, and I must have hit the food bag, because the trap door closed so hard and fast, it jammed on the spike, and I couldn't get the door open. I was stuck, and there was no one around. And no one came around for about an hour. Then some guy driving a loader pulls up. Even he had trouble, and it must have been another twenty minutes before I got out of there."

When Toronto Sergeant John Irwin was a cadet, he'd worn the same uniform as a real cop, the only difference being the word "cadet" sewn on and the absence of a gun. In his newly minted constable role, the addition of the gun made him uncomfortable.

About three weeks after he started as a real cop, he and his partner were cruising when they got a call about a jeweller having been shot in a robbery attempt. Twenty minutes later, they were behind the culprit's car. His partner made him stop and switch positions, so that the older guy was driving; it bugged him, but he knew it was because the veteran didn't want John to have to handle split-second decisions in a high-risk situation.

"We squeezed the guy against the rail; I was holding my gun between my legs and shaking like crazy. I realized that wasn't the best place to have the weapon, so I pointed it at the driver of the car, now stopped, and I'm yelling at the guy: 'Keep your hands up, keep your hands up,' at the same time wondering if I could ever shoot someone. If his hands go down, there's only one place to aim—his head—but can I do it?

"My partner was walking around the patrol car, also aiming at the guy, but it struck me that my job was to protect him. If I'm not holding it together, my partner dies. I'm his keeper, almost his caregiver, if that makes any sense. We're talking maybe twenty, thirty seconds, but it felt like twenty minutes." It ended peacefully, but the lesson stayed.

Peggy Gamble, now an OPP sergeant, remembers learning the hard way.

Someone walking along the highway looks innocent, but walking on the highway is an offense. She'd stopped, told the guy to get in her back seat—and there was no screen between the front and the back—she didn't search or cuff him, intending to give him a lift off the road. She ran him through CPIC (Canadian Police Information Centre), and the call came back through her earpiece that he was wanted, and flagged violent, including assaulting a cop.

"He was big, almost six foot three, and weighed about 250 pounds. Now I had to arrest him and take him in."

She knew that he'd figure it out if she drove straight to the office, so she quickly ran through her options. "I knew there was a gas station near us, it always had a few guys hanging around." Casually, she told the dangerous passenger that she needed to get gas and took the next exit. There were two men there, on duty, that night; so she got out of her car and let them know what she was about to do, asking them to watch her back while she took him down.

"I asked him to get out of the car, and kind of blocked him as he did, so that I could turn him around and get the cuffs on him. They barely fit his wrists, but I got it done, and got him back in the car, at which point he really went berserk."

That, too, was a lesson that lasted. Now nobody gets in her car without their bag going in the trunk, without a personal search. Interestingly, it never occurred to her to pull her gun, since "he wasn't posing a threat at the time."

Vancouver Police Constable Al Arsenault tells me that "coning" is a term police use: "It's when you take someone down so hard and so fast they end up looking like a conehead; you just flatten them without mercy. With our justice system, it may be the only punishment they'll see. You never really know what kind of weapons robbers might be carrying, even the B&E guys have screwdrivers and knives."

Susan McCoy was asked, just a few years ago, if she'd ever been shot at. "Yes, three times," was her answer.

"And then I had to think about it. I thought in the first incident, shots were fired at me, it felt that way. But when I went back and really remembered everything, they weren't, not at me. It was soon after I first started [1975], I drove up to a restaurant, the first officer on scene. There'd been a report of shots fired, and that was all I knew, though we found out later that, as a result of a love triangle, this man had put six bullets into the head of the male victim.

"As I was getting out of the squad car, this man is coming out the front door, and he turned and pointed his gun at me. I shouted at him to drop the gun, and I couldn't even hear my own voice. I thought, not loud enough. I had no idea if his gun was loaded. Why I never shot the guy, I'll never know, but I yelled again, and he dropped it.

"I never talked about it, just gave evidence in court, just facts. I couldn't talk about how it felt, because I was afraid they'd think I was weak or too emotional. I couldn't tell my parents, because they'd want me to quit. And I couldn't tell my partner because he might think I was afraid of the job.

"We had another call some years later, unknown disturbance, we drive up and this guy—who's just generally pissed off—breaks his window and starts firing at us. Right away we dive for cover and thank God he's a bad shot. And because he's a bad shot, you're really not supposed to react, stiff upper lip and all that. Again, there's no talking about it.

"The third time was a domestic call that was settled with

an arrest. The wife had gone to a neighbour's, and the husband just decided to go shoot out in the back yard, sending her a message, I suppose, that he had a gun and would use it. I have never, ever wanted to fire my gun. I never even wanted to take it out of its holster. I never have fired it."

Karen Bell has never fired her gun at an individual, although she's had to point it a few times and even had to use it to kill dangerous dogs.

"This reserve guy, wanted for something or other—I'd dealt with him a month before—took off into the bush. Then I see him; he's a passenger in a car I pass. The driver doesn't know what the hell's going on. When I try to stop them the guy takes off into the bush again. This time I call for the OPP dog and handler, and the two of us start tracking this guy. Eventually he ran out of wind, and we came up on him sitting on a big log. He had thirteen previous convictions, including "assaulting police." I had my gun out for that take-down. When we searched him, he had a chainsaw chain wrapped with tape in his pocket. If I'd gone after him alone the first time, he would have whipped that out at me from behind a tree and pretty much taken my head off."

Both Karen Bell and Jeff McArthur were members of different Emergency Response Teams, although Karen had to give it up—time considerations, once the aboriginal police force was created, independent from the OPP—which still rankles.

Jeff liked the idea of the training and the challenge, and

that "all the guys on the team were high flyers." Once a year, the ERT would host gruelling tryouts for whatever spots on the team might be available. The team itself votes on who gets in.

"It's old-boy but it has to be. You may not be team oriented, and you've got to function as a team. They want to know your work ethic, because you still have to do your regular job; this is only part time. They want to know your reputation."

He was sent to a five-week course in the Ottawa area. "There were guys you flew in with on Sunday who were flying home on Tuesday. They didn't make it through the first day; they couldn't cut the physical tests. Maybe a quarter didn't make it."

They were using a 9-mm semi-automatic, and they had to learn to shoot with these. One of the test exercises involved going into a room where six pictures were pinned to a bulletin board, and two of those pictures would have Xs on them.

"You've got twelve to eighteen seconds to commit that to memory, then you're taken to another room, where you have to kick down the door, enter, and confront six targets in full silhouette. You have six seconds to identify the two bad guys and put two shots, a double tap, into each."

Jeff passed that test. The teams are then divided into snipers and assaulters. He's an assaulter. Snipers get some distance, but it's the job of the assaulters to break down doors in hairy situations, to be the first in. The trick lies in controlling the "flight" part of the fight/flight response, acknowledging and learning to control your fear. At times like that, you revert to your training.

"A cop is one of the few people out there who can't run away. Sometimes it's important strategically to disengage, or re-position yourself, but even then you don't leave the scene. Flight just isn't an option. And that almost goes against human nature. After a few incidents that go down the way they're supposed to, without a hitch, the way your training said they would, you start feeling more confident. You've got to keep positive thoughts and a winning attitude."

Toby Hinton, now a Vancouver constable, sums up the life: "For me this was as good as it gets. You see people going over to the dark side; you're pretty active through your whole shift. There's almost a prestigious credibility in the force towards the beat constable. I'll always be grateful to the force. It created almost a totally different person from the raw material they started with. I love it—everything about it—from the adrenaline blasts to the melancholy aspects of driving around in the pissing rain."

WORKING UNDERCOVER
"I never dressed like a tramp, never did the hooker stuff"

Pretty much everyone I've talked to has done a stint of undercover work.

Karen Bell remembers: "They used all the new PWs—they don't call the men 'police guys' but the women are 'police women'—to pose as hookers. I was really nervous the first couple of times out, wasn't sure how to dress or what to say. We weren't allowed to name a price or suggest a sexual act. The john had to do that. There were two officers sitting in the dark in a car somewhere, and my signal for the bust to go down was to run my hands through my hair. They didn't do role-playing in school; that would have helped. All the real hookers knew I was a cop, but they didn't seem to mind as long as I wasn't working their corners. I was taking bad apples off the street."

They'd do about two busts an hour. Karen's backup team had to do the paperwork, give the guy a ticket to appear. Most pleaded guilty—she had to go to court only twice that she can remember.

There wasn't a lot of training in the early days. Karen remembers spending a week at a course where constables were taught what the drugs looked like, and what they cost, then being sent out to make buys on the streets, in alleyways and bars. She was really good at it.

"For some reason, certain women can only successfully buy certain drugs. Black undercover women could only get cocaine; I could get anything. So I got utilized a lot." She knew that cover stories should be as close to the truth as possible, so as not to trip yourself up.

"I played the 'stupid Northerner' to the hilt, an addict with a boyfriend who also used, to account for the frequent purchases."

She was sent, wired, into a crack house in Toronto's Parkdale district. "No firearm, no badge, no idea who was in the house, what kind of weapons they had. I was told, try and make a buy. All that was protecting me was a code word that would bring the backup team running. This humongous black guy answers the door. I buy some dope, then a lady comes up and tries to get me to go further into the house. I figured they'd either made me or had suspicions, so I made an excuse and left, heading up the street to where the van was. In seconds I knew I was being followed, so I crossed the street, towards an alley. It turned out he was looking for a blow job."

She doesn't have much respect for the intelligence of the average dealer. "You'd buy from someone working undercover, then a week later, while you're in uniform, bust them, and they wouldn't recognize you. Next time you buy from them, it's 'Are you a cop? Are you a fucking cop?' Like you're going to say."

Jay Hope spent some very lonely, emotionally draining years making drug buys in small-town Ontario. He'd hang out in bars in places like Cornwall and Bracebridge, perfecting his persona as an ex-con, "Gerry," a big guy who'd worked out a lot in his cell.

"I was two people, Gerry the asshole, and Jay, the man."

He wore tank-tops, military-style pants with patch pockets, gold chains and gold earrings, and running shoes. The OPP pays for one drink an hour to a maximum of three drinks, and that's supposed to take you through from eight at night till one in the morning.

"You learn to fake it. 'Oh, no thanks I just finished one,' or 'I'm feeling a little sick.'"

Jay won the Commissioner's Certificate for bringing in one pound of 98 percent pure heroin. His friends and family tell him he was never "right" during those undercover years. He went through a period of soul searching to find himself, centre himself again.

Susan McCoy, who's very attractive and a fashionable dresser, spent nine years in intelligence, doing undercover investigative work around bikers and organized crime. Some days she'd wear her hair up, other times she'd wear a ball cap, or stick on a pair of glasses, minor changes that worked because, "People are so caught up in their own stuff, they don't pay attention. I remember this guy I'd been following for about a week. He was involved in major drug smuggling into the country, and he was missing when I came on shift, and we're all trying to find him. I went looking for him in a parking garage, but I couldn't see him there so I head for the elevator and I'm waiting for it, and who comes up right behind me? He's a gentleman, and he waves me on first, and I keep my head down, don't press which floor because I want him to show me where he's going first. He starts up a conversation!

" 'So what are you up to?' "

"I told him I'm just going to browse around, and he says, 'You must be from out of town, cause you look a little lost.'

"He starts telling me a list of good restaurants, and he adds that he's going for lunch with a friend of his at a good place across the street. Perfect."

She'd go into some pretty decent places, when they had intelligence that a target was holding a meeting there. "Of course you usually think of ratty bars and such, and overweight tough guys in leather, but some of them are quite like business people, very well groomed. I remember my partner and I had dinner in one of those places, while we were watching and listening, and our bill came to just under $200. God, you see these guys ordering Dom Perignon, and you know it's dirty money; or they're sitting there and interacting with their family—young kids sometimes—and you can't help wondering what the kids are going to think about their father when they're old enough to understand.

"Now there are the bars where the smell gets to you, dirty, slimy places. It's those places where I started to wonder why the hell didn't I become a stewardess at Air Canada? But I've had the opportunity to see the world through so many pairs of eyes. You know sometimes when you ask people how it's going, and they say 'SSDD'—same shit, different day. I couldn't live like that, in a treadmill kind of job."

Al Arsenault has an excellent take on what's necessary to be a successful undercover officer: "You've got to drop all your usual mannerisms, unlearn a lot of stuff. Lose your awareness of your power, your strong presence, your reputation, lose the sense that you're the man. You take up shuffling your feet, picking your nose like the rest of the street urchins. I find it hard sometimes to re-equip myself for my real life—it takes time to get back to who you are. I'll be walking a beat after, and not getting my customary respect, treated like I'm weak or something, and then I'll realize I'm still half not here; it's like, Oh ya, I'm the man."

For John Irwin, now a Toronto sergeant, when he started undercover, there wasn't much in the way of preparation. Now there are some courses, but most people don't get to take them.

"I finally just got my head into it, worked out my own profile. They do give you some ideas of the people you're targeting. But it's not a science, it's a constant flux, you're always adjusting to the circumstances around you. It's the little things, body language, the talk you talk. Most police officers fit a mould, white guys, six feet tall, 180 pounds. I'm six foot, but I'm skinny, maybe 150. But I'm going to stand out if I'm trying to buy in a Hispanic or Black neighbourhood, so I have to find a way to overcome the immediate perception of difference. So I might pretend to be a university student with a habit or someone living really close.

"After the first buy, they tend to relax and accept you. If you spend a long time in a situation, it's a little unnerving, and you may have some concern about how they're going to think and feel. You've been friends, sometimes though part of that friendship is false, there is a degree of feeling a little bad, but you've got to say: Wait. That's my job. You're a dirty rotten drug dealer, and you're going to jail. I remember this one guy, I liked him as a person, we talked philosophy together, but I didn't like what he was into. We can't lose sight of the fact that our job is catching and convicting these guys."

It is interesting, this awareness John and Al share about having to give up their own sense of personal power to credibly pass as a person on the margins. And they're right. Go into any doughnut shop in a "depressed area," grab a coffee and a cruller, and watch how your presence affects the action. That you don't belong will be abundantly clear, not just by the way you dress, but by the sense of entitlement the middle class seem to carry with them, their visible good health and good teeth, the way they use their voice, their manners, their reluctance to sit at a table covered with grime. If it's an especially busy shop, where drug traffic is high, you'll be shot paranoid looks that will escalate the longer you sit.

Poor people tend to keep their heads down, try quite hard not to pay attention to what's going on around them. They walk in more of a trudge rather than confident strides.

But that's on the margins. In 1978 Margo Boyd got sent to the drug squad to do some undercover work, which caused some resentment from her peers.

"I never dressed like a tramp, never did the hooker stuff, I just wore what I'd wear on the weekends. I remember working on a cocaine bust in Yorkville. I'm sitting with an informant and two Iranians, one of whom is very romantic and tries to take off this ring I wore on my wedding finger, using butter, trying to get it off while telling me: 'We're going to Paris, you and I.'

"For a few minutes I was so excited! Paris! What will I wear?

"He was wealthy as stink, but of course I never went with him, and actually, he didn't get to go either."

Margo worked clubs like the old Elephant Walk at Queen and Bathurst. It was impossible for the uniforms to get in. They had a locked front door, a real fire hazard, with a peep-hole so they could see who wanted in. The first time she went with an informant, then established herself over time as a regular, not even buying drugs right away.

When people got used to her, she bought cocaine from different dealers at the club, and the night of the take-down, the police stood out of sight of the peep-hole while she stood brightly and expectantly in full view.

"They arrested a lot of people that night."

Al Arsenault also did "cell work."

"You're there to try and get the prisoner to talk. I'm a pretty good actor, and I had long hair. You get a bit apprehensive, of course: You never know if the guy you're sharing a cell with is a murderer or a wingnut. It can take a couple of hours or a day to get what you need.

"Sure you feel like a rat after. Here this guy spills his guts to me, and I turn around and use it to give evidence against him. It's not my nature, you know? But then you tell yourself: He's a bank robber. Fuck him."

There are consequences, career and life consequences, to spending too long undercover. Margo, Jay, and Susan all became aware of this.

Margo's mentor in the force felt that her going into the drug squad had been a career mistake, even though it was exciting and unsupervised a lot of the time—where you set your own hours and hung out in bars—you didn't get the chance to develop the discipline and the investigative skills to get ahead.

"It was almost more an acting role than a police job."

Jay agrees and counsels young black officers that investigation, rather than undercover buying of drugs, is the better route to take. For Susan, "It was, at times, great fun, like acting. When you succeed at bringing in a great bunch of information, the next few days you just feel like you're in a movie, everything's so exciting and adventurous. But we'd get very isolated, what with the hours we worked, the team became your family. You'd finish at 4 a.m., go to one of the guy's houses who was still single, sit in the backyard—rum and coke and red wine were really popular—and rehash the whole day and get shit-faced. Nobody wants to know they're drinking too much, you know, it's 'If you have a problem then so do I, and I don't want to believe that.' There's all the usual excuses, too; no one understands the job but us, or I don't want to take the job home. You pretty well keep the same pattern on your days off, a glass of wine turns into a bottle."

I've seen the same thing with institutional health and childcare workers—it may be related to frontline work with people generally. With feelings of frustration, resentment, and powerlessness building up, directed towards superiors or at the people you're forced to deal with on a daily basis, drinking becomes a bonding ritual; almost always done to excess. An excuse to let go of tightly gripped emotions.

Al Arsenault enjoyed being part of a covert strike force

for two years plus, keeping an eye on known offenders like bank robbers and break-and-enter specialists, sometimes staking them out for weeks at a time before a gang would make a move.

"It showed me another side of policing that even other police don't know anything about—ways to attack the criminal element without them even knowing about it. You're given resources, highly technical stuff that the average street cop never gets his hands on. For instance, I could be watching you right now—for God's sake, Pat, put some pants on—and you wouldn't know it. Say you want to watch someone on the 32nd floor of an apartment building. You drill a tiny hole from the apartment next door, run a feed line and a camera, while three blocks away audio/visual is playing to the cops. It's a little creepy and voyeuristic, but when all else fails, a parabolic mike, a high-powered camera, can get police what they need. The average person need not fear that kind of thing; you've got to jump through a lot of legal hoops to even get permission to do it."

Damn.

PROMOTIONS, BARRIERS, AND CFLS

"Now I can sleep my way to the top, too"

Promotions are the source of much internal rancour. There is a distrust of the promotion track, whether they're white, or women, or visible minorities. That promotion track is often seen as different than real policing, involving more public relations than public protection.

Al Arsenault declares himself "a member of the CFL club—Constables for Life." He says this with considerable pride, as a worthy alternative to climbing the ladder of "suck-cess."

"I hate the ass-licking system. I'm happier speaking my mind than being someone's boy. I take pride in being a street cop; I love arresting bad guys. I don't want to supervise someone else doing the fun stuff."

John Irwin agrees that being a member of the CFL club is honourable and fulfilling and that we may be mistaken in how we market the police force.

"We say it's a profession, with great opportunities for advancement, and people get angry when promotions are so limited, and those who get promoted are not always seen to have won this on merit. We should market being a constable as a great job, in and of itself. Which it is."

Al adds: "I've had to battle that for years: If you're not promoted after ten years, they start to look at you as if you're weird, like you need more motivation or something. It *is* a career, being a street cop, and a damn good one. It's also good for young constables to realize they don't have to chase that carrot [of promotion] around."

Jay Hope made corporal after five and a half years as a constable—before, he likes to point out, efforts at equity on the force. However, he adds, "You do hear grumbling that every jump in rank is because you're black."

If you find yourself left behind, or failing a sergeant's

exam for the third or fourth time, it is, I suppose, some comfort to point to colour or gender—rather than yourself—as the reason.

As a seven-year constable, Ken Higgins, deputy chief of Vancouver Police, found himself marking sergeant's exams. Every effort was made to keep the exams anonymous, so that the results are seen to be fair and not influenced by the marker's personal likes or dislikes. Those who pass the exam never query the results; those who came close were permitted to ask, and be told, where they went wrong. Ken found himself facing a corporal who had failed—criminal law was apparently not his strength—who was "unprintably personally offensive."

To Ken, even the most lenient interpretations of the corporal's test answers wouldn't have allowed the guy to pass. The personal nastiness, aimed at Ken, of the man's reaction was profoundly upsetting. Ken's wife assured him that he'd done his job, that he couldn't just give marks away. And the next year, Ken found himself a little more hardened, a little more determined to uphold the standards he believed in, with no exceptions, never playing favourites.

In Susan McCoy's fifteenth year, she was promoted to sergeant, the only woman out of seventy-five promoted at the time. She remembers one individual who had a reputation as the in-house jerk, coming up and saying: "I just want to congratulate you on your promotion."

"I looked at him for a minute, and I thought, maybe he means it, maybe he's not such a jerk. But then he goes on: 'Do you want to know why I'm pleased women are being promoted? It's 'cause now I can sleep my way to the top, too.'"

Margo Boyd laughs, remembering the resentment when she was placed first on the promotion list for Inspector: "I had to tell them I'm first on the list because it's in alphabetical order!"

It seems that being recognized early in your career by superiors is important for promotion chances, which happened to Bill Currie, Mike Boyd, and Jay Hope.

Bill lucked out on a take-down. Eight months into his career as a constable (4th class), he was patrolling in his cruiser when he heard over the radio that three men had escaped from a medium security institute, robbed and beaten a guy, and stolen his car. They were armed with at least one shotgun and were driving two in front, one in back.

Bill thought to himself, if I were an escaping crook, I'd stay off the major highways. He was sitting, doing paperwork, watching traffic, the sun in his eyes, when he saw an orange-brown car, with the same two last digits (all he could catch sight of) as the licence plate of the stolen vehicle. Unfortunately, there seemed to be only two men in the car, but he followed them anyway, his instincts tingling.

Eventually they turned into the driveway of a house whose owner Bill knew, and Bill thought he'd gotten carried away, at least until they smashed right into the homeowner's car, and three guys, one with the shotgun, piled out. And when the homeowner came out to investigate, he was right between Bill and the bad guys, who used the opportunity to escape into a neighbouring field. Bill excitedly called into dispatch, saying he had the bad guys on the run, calling for backup. No you don't, said dispatch, certain he was in the wrong area to have located them.

"I was lucky, the other guys on my shift believed me and came on the run. I remember I wasn't fully trained in the use of a shotgun, but as my three buddies pulled up, one tossed me a shotgun and shells, and I was loading it on the run."

The bad guys surrendered, and Bill was promoted to constable 1st class.

Sometimes, early notice might not lead to actual promotion, but may help to win a plum assignment.

Margo Boyd was the first woman in Canada to be permanently assigned to the Homicide Squad, around 1982. "This was the premier unit, an elite squad, with no women. I was still a constable, hadn't yet put ten years in. David Boothby [Toronto's recently retired police chief] and I partnered for a while, and of course that's where I met my husband."

Margo feels one of the reasons it took so long for a female to break into homicide is that too many women police officers are happy with the pink ghetto, they don't find the "real police" lifestyle attractive, and don't mind being—say—secretary to the chief, while Margo wanted to be in the middle of the fray and didn't mind at all being called at 2 a.m. to attend a scene.

"Of course, there's still a lot of sexism, but I've got my homicide ring." That's said with the satisfaction and pride of a Superbowl winner.

Mike Boyd didn't wait to be noticed. He wrote to his inspector with a suggestion of how to conduct investigations.

After completing his training, Mike spent one year in uniform, then moved to "old clothes"—what "plain clothes" were called at the time. It meant that he looked after such things as licensed premises—was liquor being served in a proper and orderly fashion. He might also deal with criminal matters, such as sexual attacks, car thefts, and break-and-enter. It was a rare opportunity for a new constable with only one year under his belt.

"Here I was, as a twenty-two-year-old, writing to my inspector, suggesting that the rash of B&Es could be stopped if it was put under one investigator, instead of treating each of them like separate crimes. I got the assignment, carried out the detective work, and was successful."

Ten days after he'd put in five years, he applied for promotion. The usual time period was ten to twelve years before being permitted to apply, but his management team recommended him. He didn't make it the first time—they probably thought he was too young—but the second time, after only six years of service, he got it. He admits to encountering some jealousy from his peers.

"You'll find jealousy in all walks of life. I've never considered myself better than anyone else. I had a very strong belief in the role of police in society, and I applied myself to my work."

Bill Currie also found clearing up a rash of B&Es to be a career booster. In the Snelgrove Detachment, north of Brampton, where the OPP has a contract to do all aspects of policing for the top half of Peel Region, Constable Currie—no longer keeping his head down—was made chair of planning.

"The way things worked there, all detachment officers would come together to look at crime in the community and decide how to allocate the available resources. Meetings involving planning were somewhat foreign to the officers, as they had no real experience in it. I didn't think that the way things were done was working.

"No one really resented me chairing, because they saw it as "soft policing," which they weren't interested in. We had four shifts of officers back then, each officer on the shift being responsible for different things. Two were assigned general duty, which essentially meant major crime. With that set-up, our clearance rate was really bad, 5, 6, 7 percent. There was no real communication between shifts. For any crime in the area, we had six million suspects in all the various communities; the bad guys could come from anywhere. I remember this rash of B&Es in some big houses in Caledon. I suggested that we take two folks from each shift and have them become a unit, work around the clock, and the head of the detachment, Bob King, went for it, and six of us became the first major crime unit. Within a year, our clearance rate was 45 percent, a phenomenal success.

"It was a tough time, though, in terms of home life. I had to develop a list of informants, which meant giving out my pager number to all of them. I'd get calls at four o'clock in the morning: 'Need to meet you at the gravel pit.' I never really had a day off."

Bill also spent five years as executive assistant (operations) to then-OPP Commissioner Archie Ferguson.

"He brought me in the first day and kept me till he left. He was like a father to me."

There had never been an operations EA before, and Bill encountered a huge amount of resentment within the organization, "that a low-life like me would have the opportunity to influence command decisions. I remember a deputy commander calling me in and saying to me, 'I want to tell you right off the bat that I don't like you, but you're smart, so let's get on with it.' I was blamed by some for hampering their chances of promotion, but the ones doing the most bitching got the promotions they wanted."

Mike Boyd was a staff sergeant in 1995, when there was a posting for the job of deputy chief. He applied, but felt his chances were so remote he told no one but his wife. He was the first candidate promoted, jumping five ranks, under the new system of competency-based selection criteria, instead of the old system of number of years put in.

"It seemed bizarre at the time. I still can't believe it. One day I'm a staff sergeant, the next I'm a deputy chief sitting in a room with the command group."

When the media announced that Christine Silverberg had been selected as Calgary's new police chief (1995), Christine was still working as deputy chief for Hamilton-Wentworth. She had calls from members of the Calgary media about a body outline—like homicide draws around a murder victim—left outside the door of police headquarters, painted pink. She gives a somewhat tortured, if not disingenuous, explanation these days about what that meant.

The headquarters of the Calgary force is in a large office tower, with other businesses, called the Andrew Davidson Building, which has balconies down one side. There was a saying in the force that when someone didn't get an expected promotion, they'd jump from one of those balconies. Christine has been told that it was simply a jokester's way of making the point—that they'd be reacting to the disappointment in the "traditional" way, and, besides, homicide always uses pink.

There's another interesting, and unintended, consequence of promotion or change at the top, as Bill Currie learned when Commissioner Archie Ferguson retired. Bill knew that his position of operations executive assistant to Ferguson "wouldn't ultimately do me any good: When the team leader goes, so does the team."

As Chief Boothby prepared for retirement, Margo Boyd faced the same situation. No matter who was hired (and her husband, Mike Boyd, was one of the short-listed candidates, along with Bill Currie), her position as director of corporate communication for the chief was fast becoming untenable.

"If Mike had got it, that would be a no-go for me in this job; and if Fantino was hired, he wouldn't want the wife of one of his deputies giving him advice."

Christine adds: "Police officers spend years and years building alliances within the force, but if someone is brought in from elsewhere, all the 'owe-me's' collapse."

RIOTS AND OTHER INCIDENTS
"All the frustrations we got rid of"

Al Arsenault faced his first riot in the early 1980s in a place called English Bay, Vancouver, where a "bunch of out-of-towners were partying on the beach, setting fires, and throwing rocks. There were thirty of us and three thousand of them. I was scared shitless. The second time was 1994, the Stanley Cup riots. This time I was a seasoned vet, well trained and well equipped. I had a better understanding of the nature of crowds and instigators. Thousands of people were pouring in from the SkyTrain, just wanting to cut loose. It was fun. They offered us post-traumatic counselling after, but who needed it? All the frustration we got rid of, the sense of finally getting your licks in. Police were 'slapping' the rioters and you know what? Hardly anyone complained because the public had absolutely no sympathy for them; they'd done more than a million dollars worth of damage, and no one really wanted to admit having taken part."

Jay Hope is a tall and imposing figure, and he radiates ambition. He didn't have nearly as much fun. "I knew when I woke up that morning at 4:45 a.m. that it would be a difficult day. I was in charge of incident control. I've been at promotion boards where guys are asked what's the biggest incident in their career. Guys remember, like the boomers remember where they were when Kennedy was shot, and they say they were really scared."

I remember that day, too, watching from home, as the Ontario Public Service Employees union and their many supporters tried to shut down the legislature by preventing the Harris Conservatives, many of whom had been bused to Queen's Park from another location, from entering the building. This was the culmination of all the bad feelings that had been in play since the neo-conservative, union-bashing government had come to power.

Jay continued: "I remember all the yelling, with this eerie quiet in the centre. It's key to be seen to be in control; I'm supposed to be directing this from the back. Our job was to create a safe corridor so the politicians could get from the bus they were in to the inside of the legislature. We accomplished that.

"Cops are always outnumbered in these kinds of situations. There were forty of us and hundreds of demonstrators. If the crowd was serious about overwhelming us, that would have been it. But it never happens."

There was a lot of pushing and shoving by all parties, and the media was right on top of it; suddenly a guy was down on the ground, apparently hurt. Jay says, "You could hear the demonstrators yelling at him to stay down."

It was a great photo opportunity.

Nervous employees inside the legislature talked to television cameras of being really startled, indignant, and fearful as Jay's team, preparing to go outside, started banging their batons on their shields, jogging down the corridors and down the stairs.

To Jay, it's what the team does "to prepare for the task at

hand, to get the team ready. Before you go into something like that, you're buzzing with nervous energy, tapping on the shields is a way of focusing. As well as giving a warning to those demonstrators that you're coming."

Bill Currie was in Aurora, twenty-five miles north of Toronto, constantly on the phone with Jay that day. "Jay's a trained incident commander, one of my best officers. I knew there'd been an altercation in one of the lines, and that Jay had actually talked to the person who got hurt and didn't want to get up. About one o'clock in the afternoon, Jay reported that the MPPs were inside the legislature and grateful for the protection. I went out to play hockey that night at St. Mike's, and I get a call from the commissioner, who's at home watching the news. And he suggests I do the same.

"That clip shows the guy lying on the ground. They didn't show the clip just before that where the police are asking him if he's all right."

The citizens of Ontario were appalled at what was happening on the grounds of their legislature, and the swinging of batons and screaming and pushing and shoving were very un-Canadian. It was pretty dramatic, and a little overplayed.

Bill Currie says, "We've certainly had the same or worse occur in other parts of the province, without the media blowing it up. To me, the reason it got to people had more to do with the stage—Queen's Park—and the costumes than the play itself."

He points out that the costumes—riot gear—haven't

been seen very often by Torontonians. There was an inquiry, and Jay, as the point person, figured if he was going south, he was going south.

"I took responsibility for what had happened, credit for the good, blame for the bad." Nevertheless, he figured that would be the end of his promotion opportunities. No incident commander "had ever been so vilified as I was."

There were even racially hateful calls to his home, which disturbed him a lot. And calls and e-mails from other forces telling him what a great job he'd done.

Jay spent three days being grilled on the stand. The inquiry's final report blamed pretty much everyone involved, so that the issue died as fast as it had come up.

"The original sin was the union escalating the demonstration and contributing to the reactions of Queen's Park spokespeople and the police. It certainly raised my profile for a while. And I'm glad no one wrote a report saying Hope is a horrible person."

He's still quite raw about the treatment he received from the press: "You'd think it was Jay Hope vs. Democracy."

Jay says he was surprised later at the actions of the RCMP sergeant (Hughie) during the OPEC demonstrations in Vancouver. "I thought to myself, he should have seen, should have learned from what happened to me. I've been consulted by other incident commanders, and what I tell them is simple: 'Do anything other than getting people injured. Do not in any way engage the crowd. It's absolutely and totally not worth it.'"

The most remarkable result in my eyes is that his

superiors didn't do what they always seem to do when controversy erupts—throw him to the wolves. And when Bill was promoted out of the Greater Toronto Area, Jay was awarded his position.

SUPERVISION AND CHANGE
"This is what they really feel; this is what they really think"

I have worked as a facilitator with the staff of psychiatric facilities. Problems sometimes occur in institutions or agencies around the way they relate to my community of psychiatric survivors. Assumptions, presumptions, and plain prejudices can and do affect all kinds of "therapeutic relationships." Facilitating these groups can be very difficult and emotionally demanding, requiring huge efforts of tolerance and calm in the face of much—mostly unintentional—provocation. As the "representative supplicant" requesting change in attitudes, I've discovered that it's important to first get those attitudes on the table, and the best, most effective way of doing that is to declare a kind of amnesty, where no one will be attacked for saying what they really think and feel.

Once I say that, however, it means listening to all kinds of button-pushing crap before beginning to address the systemic attitudinal problems. It can really leave you shaking your head at the end of the day, wondering what chance we have of being seen as people first, rather than living, breathing diagnoses? Indeed, what chance have we of reclaiming our lives from professionals, who can't quite see we're entitled to do just that? It certainly leaves you few illusions.

Jay Hope wanted very badly to become the first black homicide inspector, but he had a call from the deputy commander asking him to handle the new employment equity office.

"I told him I didn't want to be heralded as The Black Officer shaking the bushes to bring in others to the job."

His answer from the deputy: You owe the department.

Even so, it turned out to be a great move for him. It was a small unit, only four people, and they "had such fun, we saw ourselves as the outsiders." For those in other institutions, a lot of it wasn't fun at all.

> The first day Anthony Weekes started working as a corrections officer in Toronto, he was greeted with a racial slur. Seventeen years later, rampant and systemic racism persists, Weekes and other black corrections workers told a news conference yesterday. And they say neither the government nor their own union has done much to stop it. . . . From racial slurs and Ku Klux Klan signs scribbled on prison walls to denials of promotion, the workers say they've paid a price for the colour of their skin, and a dearer price for speaking out.
>
> "Our careers are done," said another guard,

> Anthony Simon, 54. He said his car was smashed after he complained. "This is the reality of the society that we live in . . . that when we speak up for our own, when we speak up for our rights and justice, we pay the price. . . ."
>
> Anthony Garrick, 41, who started working at the Toronto youth detention centre in 1986, has been active on the ministry's anti-racism committee and represented the union on race issues. "It's very difficult because you're addressing the problem while being victimized."
>
> The managers who are supposed to implement anti-racism policies in the workplace are among those who either overlook the racism or practise it themselves, Garrick said. ("Black Prison Guards tell of Workplace Racism," by Colin Perkel, *The Toronto Star*, 7 April 2000, p. A28.)

Jay continued: "We'd conduct small police focus groups, where we heard a lot of crap about equity lowering the standards. They didn't hold back because I was black. At the end of the day, I'd be so drained. I'd think: This is what they really feel, this is what they really think. Blacks, Chinese, women: I don't want to partner with one of them! At my level and rank, I don't hear much of that anymore, but from the young constables in ABLE, I know things haven't changed much. I go down to New York to visit my wife's family, and sometimes I'll go on rides along with the police there. They have many more black supervisors and detectives, it's just accepted, and yet we're supposed to be the better country in terms of lack of prejudice."

When Christine Silverberg went to work for Hamilton-Wentworth as deputy chief, the Ontario government had just passed employment equity regulations, and she was asked to go to all the divisions and teach employment equity. She says she resented this; it wasn't a great introduction to the people on the force.

I suspect that both Jay and Christine had a problem with "linkage," that although they believed in the regulations they were required to teach, they didn't want to be branded as beneficiaries of the process, which neither were. But it shows just how destructive resistance to change can be, especially on those who are seen to be a part of that change.

Something else that police find destructive is having a bad supervisor in charge of the squad.

Susan McCoy spent time as a uniform road sergeant.

"It was weird being back in uniform. I'd been out of it so long, doing undercover, and the paperwork was also new. I told my forty-five member squad: 'I'm not about to say I know better than you; we just have a job to do, together.' After completing my first year with them, I thanked them for all their support. Management didn't like that, they thought the squad would lose all respect for me. But I knew at next year's anniversary, I'd be thanking them again."

In her new role as facilitator, Susan asks her classes

every now and then: "When's the last time your boss or unit commander told you: Good work? It just doesn't seem to happen. Our greatest resource is our people, and what are we doing to take care of them?"

Susan believes we need to look at supervision in the field: How it's done; is it done?

"We need increased accountability. It might be good to have something called 360-degree supervision—what Al Arsenault and Toby Hinton are trying to get in Vancouver—where, say, myself as sergeant would be evaluated not just by the staff sergeant but also by members of my squad and my peers. I don't know anywhere that's being done at the moment. Every station has its people who just coast, called slugs, and they tend to bring down everyone else. While others are working hard, they're just twiddling their thumbs. It's, 'As long as I don't get myself into serious shit, I have a job for life.' We need to have supervisors who are present, on the road, and actually holding people to account."

When Bill Currie took over command of the Greater Toronto Region, he instituted a program he called "All Hands on Deck."

He told me, "We have more traffic on Highway 401 than on California's Santa Monica Freeway. We deal with a half million calls a year. There is resistance to change, so that if you want to introduce anything new, you give the reason, you do it yourself, and you show results. I think a simple message is the best message. If you have a gun and a badge, you're on patrol in the morning and evening rush hour, and that includes me. Paperwork and other office stuff is conducted from 9:30 to 3:00. At first, they thought I was crazy, but now it's as though I've rejuvenated careers, strengthened the common bond. We all have coffee together after patrol and it's fun, lots of dark humour."

In September 1995, his force logged 15,000 hours of patrol time; by May 1999, they'd put in 31,000 patrol hours a month. No added resources. Double the service with no added costs.

John Irwin attempts to deal with supervision as well in his classes. "We're in a paramilitary, hierarchical system. With the rank system, even though we've gone a ways in eliminating a lot of the entrenched old-boy network, a bad supervisor can make life hell. When I teach, I tell the guys they have to stand up and be counted: It's not enough to say the system doesn't work. You've got to say, "Here's a fault," and work towards correcting it. You must let your squad know they can rely on you, that you won't waffle, won't leave them hanging. Sometimes even a bad decision is better than no decision.

"If there's a problem with a platoon member, deal with it. People typically shy away from that, but if you have twenty-two people, and one or two of them are problems, you have twenty people aware that you're not dealing with the guys."

John had worked 55 Division, traffic, and as a newly promoted sergeant had a platoon of his own to lead. He had two guys, whom he felt were just coasting, and he confronted them, one after another. One of them threw a fit, yelling and calling him an asshole.

"I could have pulled rank, I could have had him disciplined—gotten into a power struggle and never gotten to the issue. But he was upset, freaked out, so I sucked it in. And made my point. This guy's overweight, in his fifties, and since we talked he's been in three foot-chases, one of them he's chasing a seventeen-, eighteen-year-old who may have a gun. He's huffing and puffing, tells me after he thought he'd die from the chase, but figured if he could just fall on the guy, he'd hold him till the others caught up, and that's what he did."

John had two rules for his squad:

- We all go home at the end of the day.
- After any interaction with the public, someone from the public should be saying, "I'm glad they came today." It doesn't have to be the person directly involved, it could be the neighbour of a crack dealer who's glad to see the back of him, but someone should be happier.

"I figure, yes, we're all tarred by the same brush, but if we do twenty calls a day, and affect the attitudes of twenty people about cops, we're chipping away at negative perceptions and stereotypes."

When asked about the disillusionment that seems to hit cops between the eyes after a certain amount of years on the job, Mike Boyd says, "I have recognized in myself an ability to remain quite balanced. I don't mean to brag or come off as psychologically stronger than anyone else, but throughout my career, I've been able to remain somewhat positive rather than cynical about the public and about the police. Sure, there are people who, when reporting a break-in, may embellish—a $400 loss being jacked up to $600. When I worked on sexual assaults, on occasion a woman who claimed she'd been assaulted may have added details that embellished or twisted her testimony. My job was to figure out when and why that happens.

"Women, historically, have not been believed about such crimes. They may feel that they could themselves be blamed for placing themselves in high-risk situations. For instance, a young woman is hitchhiking on a highway. She's picked up and assaulted. She didn't tell us she was hitch-hiking, initially. She felt mentioning it would discredit her. I understand this, and we were able to move through that and apprehend the suspects.

"I never got bitter or defensive or angry. My job is to be professional, to try and address the real issues, and to try to make it right. It's quite satisfying to address wrongs that have been committed. As a result of being lied to from time to time, I knew that while I thought I was pretty good, I clearly wasn't as good as I thought. I realized I needed to be better at recognizing truth from lies and to develop ways to move people beyond that."

Mike studied at the FBI Academy, and took courses from a former Watergate prosecutor on his interviewing technique. Not everyone gets those chances.

John Irwin, a Toronto sergeant, worked in the Sexual Assault Squad (SAS), where he had a difficult time and a major confrontation over access to victims.

"I'd give my eye teeth to lead that squad—and my four back molars to run human resources. If a member of my family was attacked, I'd want to know who was going to interview her. There are some people I wouldn't want to let near her, although of course the decision would be hers. Certainly I'd take her to Women's College Hospital; they know what they're doing and would use the rape kit."

John was working a case where the victim just didn't want to talk anymore, didn't want to drag herself through the whole thing again, and the crown wanted access yet one more time.

"I said, no way, she doesn't want to."

It seemed to him that if the choice was between the crown's discomfort with the readiness of the case, and the victim's pain, the crown should be the one to feel some pain; that's what they get paid for.

He was called on the carpet and told to listen to the crown, do what they told him. He was taken off the case, and shortly after requested a transfer out.

What Mike Boyd saw as an opportunity to learn and study, other officers would use to confirm a disdain and disrespect for the victims, for the public.

Margo Boyd was promoted into the position of coordinator of sexual assaults, a position she held from 1985 through to 1988.

"When I was in homicide, we learned about profiling from John Douglas [an FBI expert], and I started doing it in sexual assaults, by hand, getting my rubber thumb going through cases to compile profiles. We were dropping the ball in so many cases—people from different divisions working sexual assault had only two weeks of training. I wrote three reports asking for a specialized squad, but it didn't happen for a long time." In her role of coordinator, and later director of corporate communication for the chief, she ran into trouble.

"To this day, people look at me like I'm a bit of a traitor, because I'd kicked the door open and wanted people to see what was going on."

Margo was even threatened by a senior officer in one division, who told her, "If I ever hear you speaking about sexual assault issues out of my division, I'll charge you."

The threatening officer, now retired, meant she had to pretty much write off all the downtown uniforms he had charge of and concentrate on the detectives.

"He believed women lied, that the charges he dealt with were just a crock. And he was mad at how badly I'd embarrassed the force. You know, if you don't believe women when they report sexual assaults, you don't search for the men who commit them."

City of Toronto Auditor Jeffrey Griffiths reported in 1999 that the Sexual Assault Squad investigated only 4 percent of the 1,600 complaints of sexual assault.

PRESUMPTIONS AND POSTURES

"Losing respect for the victim"

Whenever police are under criticism, whether caused by a shooting or inquest recommendations, someone always emphasizes more training, and that usually carries a big "politically correct" component. But police have had their fill of political correctness: Just let us do our job. They "feel they get shit from both sides, the public and management," says Susan McCoy.

Susan had gone through some serious learning and self-examination herself, which contributed to her abilities in her new role as a facilitator. She's also unpretentious. After nine years undercover, "It had gotten to the point where I wasn't quite sure who I was. It got harder to separate myself from the job."

She determined to get her life in order. She had had two marriages, both to policemen, one that lasted eight months, the other fourteen years. "I was sure that if I could just fix the people around me, parents, husband, step-children, my personal life would get a lot better."

She had a trusted friend who worked in Employee Assistance, and Susan went to her and asked if she could help find resources or programs to deal with all the folks stressing her out. "All she said was 'Certainly.' She didn't argue with me. A few days later she gave me a sealed manila envelope, not saying much more than 'Here you go.' I remember I'd taken the subway that day, and sitting there on my way home, I thought I might as well take a look, and the first paper I pulled out had a heading Adult Children of Alcoholics. At first I thought she'd made some kind of mistake, but I read a bit more and I thought: Oh my God, this is about me. Where did they get this? And I shoved the papers back in the envelope and kind of crushed it to my chest so no one else would be able to see."

After four attempts, Susan worked up the courage to start attending group meetings, and that essentially changed her life. "I realized that the only person I could change or fix was me, and that I had to give up trying to control those around me. I also brought more balance to my life, made friends outside the force, and stopped overindulging in alcohol."

She'd worked as domestic-violence coordinator, winning the job over three or four other applicants, mostly because she was the only one who'd done outside courses, pursuing credits in social work. Her job was to coordinate with seventeen domestic liaison officers from across the city.

"I tried to give them information—issues and concerns—gleaned from the sixteen committees I sat on—as well as helping civilians understand how the police work, speaking to groups of social and legal-aid workers, spreading the word. For instance, a lot of people didn't realize that calling 911 in a domestic meant that you can't tell the officer, 'I don't want him arrested.' We arrive, and if we see evidence of a criminal act, we make an arrest."

The biggest problem for most police, says Susan is "Why does the victim, the same victim, call them two, three, four times. When the victim is told she should leave the abuser, the victim says, 'Yeah, but I love my partner.' We are asked by our officers, 'Why do they keep going back?' and there's a danger that those officers could start to lose respect for the victim. Our job was to help them understand the dynamics of the situation.

"I remember this lady, Eva, I remember telling her, 'You have to do something. Every time we come back, it's worse, and one day we'll be taking you out in a body bag.' And that's exactly what happened.

"Some of the women don't want to break up their families, though I've heard it's better to come from a broken home than to live in one. Some are still holding onto their dreams and aspirations. No one says to themselves, 'I'm going out to find the biggest asshole around, and he'll thump me every day.'

"It's not simply about men beating women, it's about power and control. And there is a lot of unpredictability in domestic assaults. You never know what lies behind that door. Officers will say, 'The victim turned against me.' But we don't know what's going on. Maybe she just wanted the violence to stop. Maybe she knows that if he's arrested, when he gets out he'll hurt her worse. The victim knows very well what the abusers are capable of. Sometimes the abuser just gives the victim 'the look,' that powerful warning that we don't understand."

LABELS

"He took on the look of a Chinese war mask"

The following fax, on Toronto Police Services letterhead, arrived at the Gerstein Centre, signed jointly by Superintendent William Blair, Unit Commander, Community Police Support Unit, and Sandy Adelson of the Police Services Board.

> The Toronto Police Services Board and the Toronto Police Services are currently exploring methods that will enhance the service provided to persons with mental illness and the people, agencies and organizations that support them.
>
> We intend to focus on the following areas as they pertain to the front-line or community levels:
>
> 1. officer training
> 2. crisis resolution
> 3. establishing partnerships and coordinating resources
> 4. implementation of various recommendations
>
> We believe that you or members of your agency will provide valuable input into this process. As issues are identified, we would like your assistance by inviting you to participate in one or more consultative groups. These groups will address and make recommendations pertaining to the aforementioned issues. The recommendations will be forwarded to the Chief of Police and the Toronto Police Services Board for review and possible implementation.

> I would like to take this opportunity to invite you or your designate to attend a forum at Headquarters. . . ."

And so I attended. At meetings like that, there can be a lot of cynicism, but people come anyway, some drifting in, others rushing, in the mistaken belief things will start on time. The cynicism is an entirely reasonable reaction—most of those attending have figured out that the real impetus behind this consultation is not the police. It's the chief coroner, who is the keynote speaker.

Police, historically, have not done well in Toronto with members of the psychiatric survivor community who lose it and engage in what's seen as threatening behaviour. Some years ago, in this same building, in a boardroom on another floor, I was the only psychiatric survivor in a room full of cops and professionals called together in the wake of another shooting of a man with a schizophrenic label. I remember feeling profoundly puzzled at the purpose of that meeting, where we were addressed by a forensic psychiatrist involved in police training, in a "isn't this wonderful, aren't we on top of this" way, got to shake hands with the chief of the day, and went home. Clearly, the "community" was there for window dressing, to say a consultation had occurred.

I remember dealing with police numerous times at the Parkdale drop-in where I worked, experiencing their quite blatant resentments and characterizations of the "seriously mentally ill" as "space cadets," their complaints about being used as an ambulance for the psychiatric hospital, and how they had to get their cars washed after "because of the stink."

One Saturday night, as I was locking the door to the drop-in, a passing uniform constable said hi, and we walked together for a while.

"It must be very hard working with those people," he said to me in a soft Scottish accent.

"Not really," I answered, "I am one of those people."

His face reddened, clearly he was embarrassed, but "gathering learning opportunities where you may" is a rule I try to live by, and I assured him that I took no offense, and the rest of our chat was pleasant and, I hope, informative for him.

Another time, I was in a restaurant, having lunch with a psychiatric nurse and an old-time cop whose stomach seemed a bit larger than his brain. I finally had to walk away from the table, unable to bear his characterizations of the people who would line up hours before the drop-in opened, the cruelty of his prejudicial comments about their appearance and their intelligence, pressing every button I carry inside me.

I also remember some very gentle cops who were respectful and trying to help. They took the time to learn the names of the men and women who lived on the streets, would stop and just pass the time of day with these people, building relationships that might one day pay off, if it became necessary to take them down to Queen Street for hospitalization.

The problem was, you never knew who you'd get; it was like playing Russian roulette.

This much larger Police Services forum seems to be a more serious effort to deal with the issues.

Dr. Cairns, the Toronto coroner, follows welcoming remarks with a sobering reminder of the three-month inquest into the death of thirty-five-year-old Edmund Yu, an intelligent and likable former medical student, who was diagnosed paranoid schizophrenic.

Edmund's acute physical discomfort with anti-psychotic medication led him to refuse it, and in 1985 he had been picked up by six officers, handcuffed, and taken to the Clarke Institute. He was homeless at the time of the incident on the bus, but he had contact with a worker at the Parkdale Activity and Recreation Centre (PARC), and he had spent the previous night at the Gerstein Centre, where I work. He was shot by police on a TTC bus 20 February 1997, after slapping a woman passenger, and after everyone but he and three officers had left the bus. Edmund Yu carried a small hammer he used in his ceremonies and prayers, and that was seen as a threatening weapon.

A lot of us at the meeting suspect that what was more threatening to the officers was his identifying himself as a schizophrenic, his tendency to bulk up his appearance with layers of clothing, and his being Chinese.

It came out at the inquest that the police officer who shot him had referred to him as a "nutbar" to other officers on the scene, before the shooting occurred. Another officer "denied it was meant as a detrimental term. I guess the politically correct thing to have said was some form of mental illness." The officer said the expression is one he had heard used over the years by other officers and is intended as a quick, informative reference when responding to calls. This same officer said in statements to the Special Investigation Unit (SIU):

"Yu made eye contact with me, which is unusual for Orientals."

"Oriental people are usually very subtle in their mood changes and don't usually erupt."

"Yu had a typical yellowish pallor, but when he became angry, he 'took on the look of a Chinese war mask.'" (By Theresa Boyle, *The Toronto Star*, 9 February 1999, p. B1.)

The Chinese community rallied around Edmund's family, as did psychiatric survivors and community workers, and it was a major news story for some time. Through his sister, the family asked that, if only one recommendation was accepted, it would be mandatory crisis-resolution training for police. Mandatory, because after the killing by police of a black man named Lester Donaldson, yet another inquest jury (1994) had recommended crisis training, teaching how to de-escalate situations with disturbed individuals. But, due to budget restraints, it was stopped after one year, and only re-instated a year ago.

Although the officers involved with Edmund Yu were cleared of wrong-doing, the question of why they got on the bus at all, when Edmund was there by himself, haunts a lot of people. A man who is paranoid—for good reason—doesn't need to be facing three officers in a limited space. They should have waited him out. With proper training, they might have avoided this tragedy.

The inquest, lasting three months, cost about $10,000 a day. That kind of money would have bought a lot of training, and it seems clear: Pay now, or pay later—in human lives, in distressed cops, in community trust.

Long before taking on this project, I had attended yet another forum, and wrote the following in *NOW* magazine ("Practicing Line for Cop Audience," August 28–September 3, 1997, p.15):

> Outside Metropolitan Police Headquarters. Thinking about the killing of Edmund Yu. I've been asked to participate on a panel scheduled immediately after a performance of *Vincent*—a play put on by the Workman Theatre Project out of Queen Street Mental Health Centre. *Vincent*, by playwright Terry Watada, is based on the real-life shooting of a young diagnosed-schizophrenic male by police, when he came at them with a baseball bat. In the play, three characters—the mother, brother, and the officer who shot him—talk in soliloquies in the aftermath of the killing.
>
> Standing here, smoking and being nervous, I've come up with, and discarded, openings, mostly one-liners, mostly inappropriate.
>
> - We would like to suggest an addition to the motto

on your cars, to serve and protect and to cure schizophrenia.

- We're recommending that any members of our community wealthy enough to use the TTC wear tee-shirts reading, "Don't Shoot, I'm Medicated."

I have avoided seeing the production of *Vincent* before; I'm nervous now that it will trigger an angry, despairing reaction in me that could frustrate any real communication.

Inside, the front row of seats have been reserved for the panel, a cop, a mother, a shrink, the playwright, and me. We are within touching distance of the actors, no real distance at all. On the plus side, I can't see the men and women in uniform and plain clothes who fill the room.

Forty-five minutes go by in a heartbeat. Mr. Watada has done a very realistic job of presenting the bewildered rage and the explosion of questions rising out of the killing, mirroring the eruption of emotions in my community at the time. He assigns no blame, suggests no answers.

After the play, the mood in the auditorium is tense, thick and still. I'm never asked to go first at these kinds of things, so I'm taken aback when the moderator chooses alphabetical over hierarchical order, and I'm up. To make matters worse, the lights are still focused on the stage where we now sit, while the rest of the room is in shadow, so that I'm left feeling like a suspect under interrogation.

I stall. Clear my throat. Look out from under my hat, squinting against the glare. I know the killing won't stop until they're able to see us as people: people who are occasionally scared to death, and act out of that fear. Just as they do.

My first few sentences are about stereotyping: how they must hate it when people automatically assume —because they're police—that they're dangerous and violent. Then I find myself telling the largely armed audience about the last time I was hospitalized, how I shared a ward with a Homicide sergeant who'd suffered a breakdown. We'd hit it off over the weeks, so much so that it became the subject matter for the "therapeutic team" to discuss. They decided we were so different, he and I, that his friendship had to be pathological and put an end to it.

I talk about the dangers of listening to mental health experts, professional interpreters of psychiatric survivors, and the need to communicate with us directly. How "mental hospitals" are always reporting staff abuse by patients, whereas at the drop-in where I put in seven years surrounded by ex-patients, there were only negligible incidents. Attitude and approach set the tone. . . .

This time [the police] are actually listening in the wake of the play, they are emoting, questioning, becoming more substantial as people. It helps that there is a scattering of community workers and psychiatric survivors in the audience—that we're all

> saying the same things, all except the psychiatrist, who seems awfully quick to justify the occasional use of lethal force. I want to thank him for being so generous and understanding with our lives.
>
> There could have been a lot of finger-pointing and yelling and defensiveness, there wasn't. There was recognition that we're beyond blame here, that these tragedies have to stop. *Vincent* gave us a forum, brought us together; it's up to us to find the answers.

The Yu inquest ended, we are reminded, last April, and this May, the coroner must report on actions taken as a result of the inquest jury's recommendations. He reminds us that the coroner's office "speaks for the dead to protect the living."

BREAKING THE RULES

It is possible to see change, even though it seems to be of the "one step forward, two steps back" variety.

Lana Fredo, a survivor herself, is on the Police Services panel, talking about her training work with officers, and her take on the difficulties involved when police encounter the "mentally ill." That even though officers may think they're helping by telling someone they're taking them to hospital, it may not be seen that way by the individual. Lana explains people's feelings about medications, what some of the physical effects are. (She tells me later that in some of the classes, police officers will say—like it's statistical gospel—that a mentally ill person can have the strength of twelve normal people.)

In response to a point made about police needing to know more about the mental health system and what's available out there, Lana reminds the audience that there is no real mental health system, that it's uncoordinated, and that it's not just the police who don't know who's doing what, that often one agency will have no idea of what another agency is doing.

Anita Barnes is a worker at Toronto's Mental Health Diversion Court. She correctly lists the causes that get most psychiatric survivors in trouble with the law:

- Homelessness;
- Poverty—exacerbated by cuts to social assistance and to programs;
- Addictions—with few rehab beds available; and
- Lack of identification.

It adds up to a very real community, agency, and government failure that drops individuals through large crevices, and leaves police, who are ill-equipped to do social work, on the front line to deal with the consequences.

Having done groups at PARC's drop-in on "Surviving Children's Aid" and ways to behave when stopped by the cops—not the time to get aggressive—I suggested that agencies needed to be inviting cops in to speak about how they do their jobs, and what they feel when confronting an individual in distress. This would give those labelled "SMI" (seriously mentally ill) an awareness of the very real consequences of the wrong move at the wrong time, give them a fighting chance to get out of a confrontation alive.

It's not just the cops who need to learn, and we fail our clients if we don't consider these basic lessons of survival for those on the street.

Susan McCoy has been teaching and facilitating police officers at Toronto's C.O. Bick College, where in-house training is done, as well as being the place where Toronto officers must re-qualify annually on all use of force procedures, such as handcuffs, the baton, and the gun, as well as training human rights issues, workplace harassment, diversity, all the "isms," as she puts it. In policing, these are known as soft skills.

She figures she gets three types of people attending: "The Learner—who goes to his supervisor and says, 'give me as many courses as possible.' He wants to be there. The Vacationer—looking at four days off. Not opposed to learning, if he gets something out of it, okay, if not, no loss. The Prisoners/the Volunteered—probably been told they're a screw-up, that they're in need of an attitude change; or as part of the reaction to a complaint process, they need more sensitivity (though it's not a course in that).

"We're not there to browbeat them or to tell them they're bad cops or bad people. We bring in speakers from various communities, such as gays and lesbians, who will talk about the issues they see, as well as what it's like to 'come out' to families and friends, about the diversity of thought and opinion in their own community. And the instructors will answer police officers' questions about nudity on Pride Day, and sometimes female officers (never the men) will use that time to come out themselves, always shocking the class because the stereotype is not met by their appearance."

Susan cared enough about the force and the need for the kind of work she was doing to take the extraordinary step of breaking ranks, in public, in front of her superiors. The odd thing was, for such a momentous act, if an audience member wasn't aware of the dynamics at play, it might have passed unnoticed—just another moment of business as usual.

I was present that day, having received a call from a local activist that diversity training was on the agenda of the Police Services Board meeting at police headquarters. Susan had been increasingly concerned that the force was not putting the same value on training as she believed was necessary. Her section had gone from a maximum level of staffing of five people, to three, to two, and then one.

She'd been on her own for some time, almost a year, and had also had to deal with physical illness. Training was even shut down for awhile, due to, she thought, a shortage of officers on the street.

There seems to be an attempt to keep her from speaking or so the audience believes. Two white, middle-aged men, her superiors, sit in a huddle with Chief Boothby, which makes for the peculiar optics of three white men assuring the Services Board, and through them the public, that diversity training is well in hand. "We've resolved the staffing issue."

Susan, called up by Kyle Rae, an openly gay city councillor, begs to differ. Sitting across from Boothby, she talks about the problems with "resolved" staffing, including the fact that two of the new staff have no experience in facilitating groups.

Susan had decided to retire from the force, or she never could have done this, contradict her bosses and upset the chair, who complains about rumours flying around that there were going to be cuts. Rumours or not, there won't be cuts now.

Vice-chair Jeff Lyons recommends the hiring of one more officer to bring the total number of trainers back to five. Then it's over as fast as it's begun, and Susan is a little shaky as she returns to her seat. She broke the rules.

Nicki Casseres, a volunteer coordinator at the Gerstein Centre, has participated in diversity training at the police college for about five years, largely around gay and lesbian issues, and, at times, around mental health issues for the Gerstein Centre. She believes Susan was very brave to do what she did. She regrets that the force never admits to making mistakes, that, at times, everything seems like a cover-up.

But Nicki has seen change, even in herself. "I used to be very afraid of the cops. I came out when I was nineteen, when cops were seen as the enemy—they'd be undercover in gay bars or raiding them. I remember an incident where some women—including me—had been brutally gay-bashed by men, and when we heard the cops were coming, we all ran, we picked up some of the women who were badly injured and ran."

She finds it easier to deal with groups up at the college, where the instructors are very clear that although cops can ask whatever they want, they must show respect. It's much more hit-and-miss when she does the parades—shift changes—on crisis intervention at the individual divisions.

"It's where the cops talk about their assignments or procedures or listen to representatives from the community. If you're lucky, the person who heads the division might attend, might be receptive, and that sets the tone. But most often you're trying to talk to from five to twenty officers, who just make you feel you have to rush through your presentation, there's no time to do this, no time for that.

"It's difficult to understand that reaction, especially when you have people laughing together or reading magazines in the back. We're offering them ways of using our service so they don't find themselves going out to deal with the same individual two or three times. There can be a lot of resentment, feelings that the public expects too much of them, and that puts a ball and chain around progress. They may not want to deal with the "disturbed" mentally ill, but it's their job. They can't remove themselves from the equation."

At the Edmund Yu inquest, one of the officers involved in the shooting, in spite of spending years in the psychiatric ghetto of Parkdale, could only name one agency. As I write this, there is yet another inquest into the shooting of a "mentally ill" man by a Toronto police officer. In June, there will be one more showing of the play *Vincent* and another series of speakers on the need to de-escalate potentially violent confrontations.

Perceptions, Politics, and Publicity

"This police union executive is not running this city"

Toronto Police Service Core Values (from their Web site):

- Honesty—we are truthful and open in our interactions with each other and with members of our communities;
- Integrity—we are honourable, trustworthy, and strive to do what is right;
- Fairness—we treat everyone in an impartial, equitable, sensitive, and ethical manner;
- Reliability—we are conscientious, professional, responsible. And dependable in our dealings with each other and our communities;
- Respect—we value ourselves, each other, and all

members of our communities, showing understanding and appreciation for our similarities and differences;

- Teamwork—we work together within the Service and with members of our communities to achieve our goals, making use of diverse skills, abilities, roles, and views;
- Positive Attitude—we strive to bring positive and constructive influences to our dealings with each other and our communities.

The reluctance or inability of police to deal with systemic issues within their forces, issues like how police behave towards each other, and how, especially in "high crime areas," they interact with the public, has permitted and institutionalized the growth of resentments and grievances. Police unions have moved from simply dealing with issues of pensions and salaries and become a force within a force, which brooks no criticism of its members.

Some cops remind me of my old boarding-home owner, who had a house full of the "seriously mentally ill," and who would yell at those outsiders who would criticize how he dealt with them: "I take people no one else wants, no one else can handle. So don't tell me how to take care of them. You think you can do better? You take them."

There is a lot left unsaid these days, but those in high-crime, high-poverty areas, and those who police them, have a keen understanding of the realities.

Citizens are unhappy about the number of homeless on

the streets, about being constantly badgered for spare change, about their parks and other public spaces being used as bedrooms and toilets. They're worried about drugs coming into their children's schools. They're worried about the level of violence that creates "innocent victims." Citizens want something done. And politicians who want to get elected plug into that, promising to clean up the streets and parks and neighbourhoods.

Law and order. Tough on crime. Tough on poverty. Cut welfare rates. Reduce the number of people eligible. Increase the number of boot camps and prisons. Send single moms out to work.

Not surprisingly, this can be interpreted by cops as a licence to do the necessary. And, since no one else has been able to deal with the problem: Don't tell us how to do the job. Don't tie our hands with bleeding-heart, civil-rights legislation. Don't come after us for "excessive force."

Police unions have flourished in this atmosphere, aided and abetted by timid politicians and by their own management. Every shooting is righteous; each and every cop placed under public scrutiny is a victim of political correctness.

The attitude of some cops seems to be: "What does the hierarchy know about the streets surrounding Fort Apache, the day-to-day realities faced by the street cops?" Already fenced in and shackled by concerns around political correctness, blamed by the media for every niggling misstep, they weren't going to lay themselves open for more.

The dynamic between frustrated, angry residents, and

defensive, angry cops is a destructive one—both groups tend to blame each other for circumstances that seem to be outside their control.

Although a cynical, "street-wise" cop is often viewed with reverence by new recruits, and perhaps emulated in any community work involving frontline interactions with the poor or marginalized, cynicism in work is recognized as burn-out, and seen—appropriately—as a negative. It can mean an individual dreads going to work but can't afford to quit. That same individual may resent all the demands from clients and may view them all as undesirables trying to "put one over on him." Nothing new in programming or models is seen as positive; no supervisors are seen as legitimate and worth listening to. These individuals are certain their reality, their perceptions, are the only valid ones, and are quick to dampen the enthusiasm, energy, and high hopes of new workers.

How you feel about your work, and the people you work with, dictates how you interact with the public. Police officers can develop attitudes that everyone they deal with is either lying or stealing. Some claim it's one reason they stick to themselves.

Jeff McArthur, RCMP constable, spent four years in Surrey, and his outlook changed, leaving him with, "though this might not be the right way to put it," a generally low opinion of people there. "Your day-to-day contact seems to be only with dishonest people, in every respect. Even taking a report on a break-and-enter, you know they're not reporting exactly what was stolen. A 14-inch television becomes, for insurance purposes, a 24-inch set; a small radio becomes a stereo system. I associated with very few people outside the force. I suppose that's pretty common; no one knows what you encounter except other police. There are other professions like that, I'm sure, where you just don't want to explain everything to an outsider, where you stick to your own."

Al Arsenault, a Vancouver constable, has come to feel that policing is often baby-sitting. "Really, if people just showed some respect for the feelings of others and for property, instead of 1,200 police we'd need maybe 50 in Vancouver."

He uses the real-life example of two businessmen in the process of dissolving a million-dollar partnership coming close to blows over the disposition of a fax machine worth a couple of hundred bucks.

A bunker mentality has little to recommend it. I spent ten years in Toronto's west end, where pretty much all I saw was people in wretched circumstances, sniffing glue or other inhalants, street alcoholics attacking one another with a brutality and relish that can leave your basic faith in humanity shaken. Pregnant street prostitutes getting into cars, and sometimes not returning. It would be odd if there wasn't cruelty, despair, and crime rampant when people are already living in a hell most of us can't imagine.

My strategy, one of pure survival, was to go to a different neighbourhood, one with parks not littered with bodies, one where schoolchildren didn't have hollow eyes and no hope, where they played in the schoolyard rather than standing on the street corners trying to make money to buy dope. You can regain your perspective, although you never forget.

Cops need to break out, get out more, talk to people with other lives, other opinions, and better experiences.

Vancouver Deputy Chief Ken Higgins knows the importance of this. He'd come back from a weekend of working with air cadets, something he did on his off hours for a good twenty years, and says, "It's important to do a variety of things, bring a fresh mind from different tasks.

"I remember dealing with 'shots fired' on patrol, then coming in and listening to a complaint from one of the air cadets' mothers that her son had been forced to eat processed cheese on the weekend away. It gives you perspective, a whole different set of issues and problems."

WHO'S IN CHARGE?

"You can call me a bully"

I'd seen Craig Bromell on television, read about him in the papers, and as a result was apprehensive about sitting down with him. He was riding high when we finally met for lunch at Accents on the corner of Bay and Wellesley in downtown Toronto. In the eyes of many, he had successfully intimidated the city into a new contract with the police force, dropping broad hints about job action if their demands weren't met. He'd been widely quoted as saying, "We feel we can do anything we want."

He's a hefty guy, with a distinctly fifties look about him, even with the gray golf shirt he wears under his jacket. His abundant silver hair is swept back from his forehead, and his face sports a mustache.

I've changed clothes twice, even after I called to check whether the upscale restaurant had a dress code. It didn't, but with my limited wardrobe, I have a choice between black or blue jeans, and shirt or tee-shirt. I'm not sure what I'm aiming for in self-presentation, perhaps an air of assurance, reasonableness, openness.

Craig is greeted by name when we are seated—a celebrity is a celebrity—and he tells me to order whatever I'd like, though he himself is on a new, high-protein diet. He has a new wife (who runs her own business supplying desserts to major coffee-bar chains) and very young children he'd like to be around to see grow up.

He is surprisingly civil with me throughout our lunch, polite and helpful, but he can't help radiating menace even when he doesn't want to, it's become such an integral part of his personality.

I also find myself remembering a television piece I'd watched on image consultants who work with rap and hip-hop groups in an effort to make them appear more acceptable to the mainstream—and a particular segment where they were being taught "society" table manners, which fork to use first, what to do with the napkin.

Throughout the lunch, I keep sneaking looks to see if his pinkie finger is extended when he lifts his glass. Believe me, having had to learn this stuff late in life myself, I would have empathized with him if he had. Both of us would probably have been more comfortable hunched over a doughnut.

This was meant to be only a preliminary meeting, a chance to size up each other face to face, to establish the minimum trust level necessary to do a good interview, but it proves to be our last encounter. My follow-up phone calls and requests to meet go ignored, leading me to suspect that I've found my way onto his enemies' list.

If you've ever had anything to do with fighting injustice, whether in an agency or at work or in society in general, it's impossible not to feel—at least initially—some sympathy for him.

Craig Bromell's life might have continued on like most frontline cops—work till you're eligible for your pension—but in 1996, he and eight others from 51 Division were accused of beating up a "known" crack dealer down at Cherry Beach in an act of vigilante justice.

For six months, he endured the investigation (even his bedroom was bugged). His father was suffering from terminal cancer but was determined to hang on until his son was cleared. Bromell's eyes get watery when he tells all this; there is no question this still causes him great pain. (His suspicion that this was personal is enhanced by the fact that this particular dealer was a white guy—if he'd been black, maybe all the fuss could be viewed as public relations, but a white crack dealer? The insinuation is, who the hell would care?) For different reasons, we stare at each other, wondering.

It's hard to tell whether Craig found it upsetting that the police would take the word of a known criminal against those of the cops themselves or whether he was really innocent. The nine cops, all from 51 Division—called the "51–9," an odd cop twist on the Chicago 7—were eventually cleared. However, there is still a civil suit pending.

Bromell had organized a march of thousands of officers on Queen's Park in 1992, over new regulations on the use of force; and he'd led a wildcat strike at 51 Division in 1995, just as the new compromise candidate for chief, David Boothby, was settling into his office. There were no immediate consequences for the officers involved; a mistake that would haunt the new chief's tenure. (As one senior officer put it, if my dog barks once, and I feed him, and if he barks again I feed him again, the third time I'd better be prepared to give him what he wants when he wants it.)

Bromell ran for the president of the Toronto Police Association in October 1997, against Paul Walter, the incumbent. During our lunch, Bromell claims he was told by a reporter that Paul Walter had agreed with the chief that they needed to get rid of him. It didn't work out that way. Bromell won handily, and hasn't—to this point—looked back. And why is this?

> He knows the crap that you deal with, said one 11-year veteran of the force, speaking on condition his name not be published. In the old days, he explained, you could deal with crime on the street. If you got physical at times, the public would support that.

> Now, if somebody says you so much as laid a finger on them, you have I don't know how many groups to investigate you. And police management . . . will be after you, too, so they'll have a little feather in their cap. It's kind of hypocritical. ("He's out to rearm a force under fire," by Sean Fine, *Globe and Mail*, 15 February 1999, p. A1.)

Craig was raised middle-class in Oshawa, Ontario, where his father was vice-president of the union of outside city workers. Craig joined the police force after successfully completing training at Aylmer's Police College. From there, almost twenty years ago, he was sent to 51 Division. That's a long time to spend on the streets.

It becomes very clear during the lunch that Craig is in over his head, that's he's displaying all the signs of a man whose ego is swallowing him whole. It's like sitting with someone, knowing—though he doesn't—that cancer is eating him up. I keep wanting to interrupt him as he talks, warn him. But that's pretty silly, he wouldn't be willing to take advice from me.

In Canada's biggest city, the lack of strong, effective leadership has created a vacuum in which, in the eyes of many, the "real" chief has been replaced by the shadow chief, Bromell.

He's a controversial figure; the press uses various epithets to describe him, from thug to flat-foot emperor, and he's okay with that—he tells me he keeps every negative article written about him on his office walls.

The mayor had announced that very day that he would take the seat on the Police Services Board—the governing body for police—recently vacated by beleaguered councillor Judy Sgro. Craig enjoys displaying insider knowledge. He assures me the mayor will stay on the Board only until the new police chief is chosen.

Bromell brags that no politician has shot off their mouths about police since he announced the intention of the Association to go after, even investigate, politicians who do. He's also disdainful of the media, saying that he saves all kinds of money in advertising his positions or decisions; the media do it for him.

"Twenty percent of the people will always be against me, 20 percent will be for me, and 60 percent could go either way. It's not a one-man show, of course. We've been so successful the last two years. We really haven't had anything go against us. We've negotiated two contracts in fifteen months. We've got the best pension plan probably in Canada, and our Association is the best one out there."

Craig says he listens to his advisors and his Board. And because of that he feels protected from doing or saying the wrong thing at the wrong time. What he doesn't get is that listening only to those who think and feel the way he does is not much protection at all. He lets drop, in between other comments, that "people" are talking to him about writing a book . He's interested in the mechanics of hiring a ghost writer, and when I suggest he ought to write it himself, I catch a brief glare—he doesn't have the time.

He says that "people" are also suggesting he apply for

the chief's job. That is so over the top that I am now alarmed he believes this kind of thing. He tells me how surprised he is that when he shows up anywhere unexpectedly, ripples are instantly created, like "Oh no, what's he doing here?"

He talks about his war chest, his roster of thirty investigators—mostly former cops—and the number of lawyers the Association has standing ready.

When former provincial cabinet minister Al Leach comes over to our table, Craig doesn't bother to stand up to shake hands with the man, nor does he introduce us. He sits back like that "flat-foot" emperor accepting tribute from a peon. In case I've missed the significance of the moment, Craig points out that Leach is now involved with some kind of civic business group—subtext: "Look how terribly important I've become, even to those outside the system."

There are so many traps for the unsuspecting or the ill-prepared in the activist/organizing business: The biggest of these is overestimating one's own abilities, intelligence, and friends, and underestimating those of your opponents. What got Craig through on the street will get him killed in the corridors of power.

As we wrap up our lunch, he gives me the name and number of reporter John Duncanson from the *Star*. He likes how John portrays him, and he also gives me permission to talk to Association lawyer Gary Clewly.

A week or two later, I open the outer door to Clewly's law office. Clewly and Bromell are tight: It was Gary who successfully represented Craig against the accusations of Internal Affairs regarding the young man who says he was beaten up by the "51–9." The only people in the reception area are CBC camera and sound guys. Gary doesn't come out of his office, so I decide to be patient and simply take a seat. I've met producer Oleh Rumak before, at a public forum on "Choosing the New Police Chief," where we exchanged opinions about Bromell, mine being that Bromell would self-destruct. Rumak is doing a profile for the *Fifth Estate* and has been following Craig around. Apparently they are here to tape a telephone conversation Gary is to have with Craig. It takes what seems forever, but when they're done, Oleh reminds Gary of his appointment with me, and I'm finally called in.

Tall and good-looking, Gary comes on like a "player"—a mover. There's a distinctly American feel about him; he radiates it. Now I'm not a prima donna; I know in the scheme of things I'm a minor annoyance. I've been treated dismissively by politicians and bureaucrats in the past, but I find Gary's behaviour sets new standards in rudeness.

He asks me what I want to know, and as I start to tell him, he picks up the phone and dials out. He has at least three phone conversations as I'm sitting there, notebook and pen in hand.

Oleh sticks his head in the door to tell Gary they're clearing out, and a peculiar dance occurs. From his position behind his desk, Gary eyes Oleh speculatively and, with just a tinge of contemptuousness, throws out that Craig and he and "a friend of the Premier's" will be at a lunch meeting today.

Oleh rises to the bait, and asks, seems almost to plead, if they could possibly film the lunch. I feel momentarily depressed that Oleh is doing this; he seems to have swallowed the bait hook, line, and sinker, but that just shows how much I have to learn. Gary relents, doing Oleh a big favour, and says: "We'll be at Oro's on Elm Street, east of Bay."

"Maybe we'll see you there," says Oleh, hopefully.

This also seems to signal the end of my non-interview, as moments later Gary rises from his chair, with a perfunctory apology almost as insulting as the non-interview itself, and leads me to the door.

These guys are like the power equivalent of *nouveau riche*—crass, short-sighted, and very, very foolish.

MEN IN BLACK

"To bully and intimidate"

On Wednesday evening, November 24th, the *Fifth Estate* aired its show about the head of the Toronto Police Association. It's immediately clear that the national stage is way too big for Craig, and he dives into the trap of being the tough, uncompromising cop revelling in his power. Indeed, so does Association lawyer Gary Clewly.

Host Victor Malarek introduces Craig as the union boss who really runs the Toronto Police Service. He asks, rhetorically, if "to protect and serve" has become "to bully and intimidate." Victor wonders if some members of the Association have become Craig's private army and points out that some of the men who accompany him from place to place have been dubbed "The Men in Black," all more or less dressing alike.

Craig and Gary are filmed at the scene of a police shooting, both showing clear disrespect and disdain for the SIU, the body empowered to investigate shootings by police.

Gary is heard calling the investigator a stooge; there's also an ominous suggestion that the process has been interfered with, that "calls were made."

Craig admits that he and "his team" went to, of all places, Los Angeles (then embroiled in the biggest corruption scandal in decades) to pick up pointers from their American brothers in the union. It was there they learned that one of the ways to get a higher profile for their Association was to target a high-profile politician and try to get him or her out, in order to keep the others in line.

"Correct," Bromell says. "I think that if you found somebody who is an enemy of the police, we don't want him around so you try and get him kicked out of office. Pretty simple, you're gonna keep all the other loud mouths, they're gonna keep their mouths shut."

Victor asks Craig if it's true that he has pretty nasty stuff on file on their "perceived enemies." Craig responds that he wouldn't tell Victor if he did, but "if we need it, we'll use it."

"Believe it or not," Craig continues, "Since we announced that private investigators are working for us, and we're gonna target our enemies, we've probably had about 120 complaints—stuff people thought we could use against them—it comes down to personality conflicts—I mean the people who snitch on politicians are other politicians—they're the worst of the lot."

Victor says: "That's pretty scary, private investigators to get your enemies."

"Why not?" says Bromell. "If anybody can give me a reason why not, I'll listen, but nobody's come up with a reason that, you know—everyone was screaming—but I can tell you since we announced it nobody's saying anything."

Politicians whom Craig doesn't like are referred to as "scumbags."

Former Councillor Judy Sgro is shown talking about a closed-door meeting of five members of the Service Board with Craig and six other members of the Association. She says she felt she was subjected to intimidating tactics, as one by one the police interrogated her about statements she'd made. She believes she was targeted because of the L.A. advice. "They had copies of everything I'd ever said in the media."

She was told that nothing said at the meeting was ever to leave the room. (When the Police Association had revealed its plans to campaign against politicians who criticized the force, Judy had said, "It reminded me of something you'd see in Louisiana, where you daren't ask the police anything, or you'll be found dead in the back of a car a week later.") Judy Sgro told me later that one of the factors in her decision to run (successfully) for a vacant seat as a federal MP was her family's concern for her safety.

Both Premier Harris and Mayor Lastman are shown

stroking Craig's ego, Lastman actually embracing him, calling him "my kind of cop."

Susan McCoy watched the show that night. She thought at first the "Men in Black" thing was some kind of joke. She couldn't believe it was for real. Her non-police friends were calling her and asking, what the hell is going on here? "It's like they want to get back to being a police force, instead of police services. Like the stereotype of a goon squad. There's no way he's speaking for all of us."

Susan doesn't attend union meetings, "All they do is drink beer, bitch, and drink some more."

Bill Currie was also watching. "I thought to myself, if I was a visitor to Toronto, a tourist, and I turned on the *Fifth Estate* that night, I would have thought they were talking about a third-world country. I never would have thought they were talking about a civilized community in a big city."

He was also disturbed at the failure of the print media to pick up on the issues raised in the show. "I only saw one article about it. You know, as a law-abiding citizen, and someone who's been here a long, long time, I don't feel threatened. If I was a member of a vulnerable community...but then, you don't really know how accurate the depiction was, you don't know what was edited out."

"The Ontario Provincial Police Association," Currie says, "is more like a family. We involve representatives in the business, offer management training for members. When we have a Mess Dinner, the OPPA is at the head table. Not that we're sucky or they're sucky. It's a way to develop future leaders from the rank and file."

Constable Toby Hinton is glad there's a union in Vancouver to look after issues like salaries and pensions. He attended a few meetings "But it's been my experience that 4 percent of the members of the union require 80 percent of its time."

He's even leery about the grievance process. "You're supposed to go to the shop steward, but you have to ask yourself, how closely is he associated with the bosses? Are promotion hopes at play? Who has loyalties to whom? I'd almost feel better with an outside, impartial arbitrator."

But the *Fifth Estate* wasn't finished with Bromell. Oleh let me know that Craig, in keeping with his character, actually liked his portrayal on the show. The CBC is planning to do a second segment on Bromell, and Oleh suggests I might want to talk to Deputy Chief Bob Kerr.

TRUE BLUE

"Find the snitch"

I had been aware that Kerr and Bromell have clashed for some time, and rumours that Craig had asked Julian Fantino, front-runner for new police chief, to fire or retire Kerr during a private meeting had become media fodder.

Adding fuel to the fire was the tragic fatal stabbing of an undercover officer by two women, and their conviction. Even more tragic was what came out, in a leak to members of the press: The officer's backup team had apparently been out drinking and attending a hockey game while putting in for on-duty pay while their partner was dying.

> Two officers working with Detective William Hancox the night he was slain went to a children's hockey practice and two bars—one in Unionville, the other in Oshawa—while on duty, according to transcripts of interviews by Toronto police Internal Affairs. . . . A police internal affairs investigation was launched after it was learned that [the two officers] were drinking while on duty the night of the Hancox slaying.
>
> According to transcripts from the probe, Hancox's widow, Kim Hancox, sought answers about why [Constable and surveillance unit member] Smith were not with her husband at the time of his slaying and why Smith's name was never mention in court. . . .
>
> [Defense] lawyers are angry because during the trial they were not provided all the details surrounding the night of the incident. During the trial, neither [of the two constables'] names were mentioned by Hancox's partners. ("Hancox probe lists officers' visits to bars," by Donovan Vincent, *The Toronto Star*, 7 January 2000, p.1.)

It is unlikely, we're told, that it would have made any difference to the deceased officer, who himself had just gone off-duty and stopped to pick up some groceries—or to the confessed guilt of the defendants. What was appalling to me personally was the sound bite from Craig about this development: ". . . A determined threat to find the person who'd leaked the information."

Boothby's reaction wasn't much better, even as he handed the file on these two cops over to another police force to investigate. He seemed to simply shrug off the idea of on-duty cops having "a couple of beers" as no big deal. Even after the initial report came in, his relief that nothing "criminal" had been done was unseemly, to say the least.

These are the representatives of the same force that has trouble with the hiring and promotion of minorities, suggesting a conspiratorial lowering of standards, and yet these men allow such a terrible stain on the honour of the force, compounding it, in Bromell's case, by going after whoever leaked it, and in Boothby's by not appearing to understand how terrible this looks to the public. Of course, there were other, more considered statements later on, but the public had had quite a glimpse into the inner workings of "Toronto's finest."

I think about how Bill Currie and Ken Higgins, almost reverently, talk about the responsibilities involved in being a police officer.

Bill says, "We're the only citizens of the land who have the power to take away a person's freedom, to exercise the ultimate act of putting someone in cuffs into the back of the squad car. Judges, juries, they're after the fact of that initial removal of liberty."

Ken Higgins remembers always an early lesson: A constable is just a citizen with a local appointment to do things on behalf of everybody else. These powers are heavily dependent on the public trust.

> The lawyers for the two women convicted of Hancox's murder say the file provides insights into the code of silence police officers tend to adopt when something goes wrong within their ranks.
>
> The file also shows how Hancox's wife, Kim, sought answers to the question of why Smith was off drinking with Manuel, a detective from the intelligence unit. She repeatedly asked for an occupational health and safety investigation into the absence of Smith and the drinking episode. ("Everybody knew officers were drinking," by Donovan Vincent, *Sunday Star*, 9 January 2000, p.1.)

Just around this time, someone claimed to have traced the leak to Deputy Chief Bob Kerr.

The *Fifth Estate* aired its second segment 19 January 2000. Most of it appeared to be a repeat of parts of the first show, with the addition of the True Blue campaign, and a powerful, brief interview towards the end with Bob Kerr.

He says, on that show, that he has heard indirectly from another officer that the Association has information on him that will be made public if he doesn't retire in March.

Kerr has a face that looks like it was chiseled out of rock. He's tall and angular and radiates strength, until Victor Malarek asks him, "Do you fear Craig Bromell?"

Bob Kerr's face starts to show the enormous strain he's

been under, over accusations that he's a snitch, accusations calculated to make him a pariah in the police community, and the long and acrimonious battle between him and Bromell. He utters a kind of crumbling. "Yes."

"You're a deputy chief and you fear him, what does that say to the public?"

"It's all very frightening."

But Kerr won't be giving into them.

The True Blue campaign was the beginning of the end for the executive of the Police Association. It was a fund-raising effort that many feared was launched to replenish the war chest of the Association and that might be used to go after politicians who were seen as critical of police. There had been so much talk of private investigators—what were they to be used for?

The Association had entered into an agreement with a telemarketing firm, where, in return for donations, the public would be offered bronze ($25), silver ($50), or gold ($100) windshield decals.

It's funny what the public gets upset about, what becomes the final straw that breaks the camel's back. During the campaign, calls to city council and the media are overwhelmingly negative. The citizens of Toronto really don't like Operation True Blue. They don't like getting soliciting phone calls, some worry about the consequences of saying no, others that cops handing out traffic tickets might not give them to cars displaying gold decals. One cop is quoted in the news saying he'd be more inclined to ticket a car with a decal, in order to show he's not influenced.

SHOWDOWN

"How will you deal with this?"

It's 26 January 2000, and it is still high noon, and there's no Gary Cooper in sight.

The level of tension at Toronto Police Headquarters rises steadily. No one's surprised that this scheduled meeting is now forty-five minutes late in starting. There are almost as many media people as there are observers in the room, and every now and then the reporters rush out to one scrum or another, catching the mayor, or the chair of the Police Services Board, or city councillors in the harsh camera lights. The Police Services Board has been under a lot of pressure to act, to rein in the Police Association executive, to force an end to Operation True Blue. The Board has dropped the ball before; the consequences of dropping it again have a lot of ordinary citizens worried.

Toronto has been through numerous changes in the last few decades. It's now not only the largest city in Canada, but also the most multicultural. It's a matter of some pride that the vast majority of its citizens, something over 80 percent, both like and respect the men and women of their police service. (Of course, we felt pretty much the same about our world-class restaurants until a series of health inspections left us all a little green.) Politicians are understandably reluctant to go up against those kinds of favourables, but they may believe they've been handed a safe issue, a safe place to draw a line in the sand.

In front of me, a member of city council jokes about

being here just to get her name off the Association's hit list, adding "There are six of us on it now."

Behind me, lawyers laugh and loudly declare their preference for sitting in the "non-scumbag" section.

The Board meeting begins quietly and goes on, in a subdued fashion, hearing from delegations, including the wonderfully plain-spoken counsellor Anne Johnston: She talks about her stunned disbelief at viewing the *Fifth Estate*, her disgust at what Bob Kerr has had to endure, about the need to rein in the Association. And goes on to say that while it's okay to be forceful in negotiations it's never okay to intimidate elected officials. (The Association had announced its intention to sue Judy Sgro for her statements on the CBC show.)

"How will you deal with this?" she is asked. Johnston says she never felt intimidated before, but now it's as though you're taking your political life in your hands, that it places you in danger of being added to the list of those targeted.

But the whole room is galvanized when the vice-chair of the Police Services Board, provincial conservative government appointee and lawyer Jeff Lyons starts to speak. It's entirely unexpected—he's seen to be as pro-police as the chair, Councillor Norm Gardner—but here he is, pounding a clenched fist on the table, saying, "Enough is enough! This has got to stop!"

Lyons says that as long as eight months ago, he'd decided to keep his distance from Bromell, that he has also felt intimidated, that he'd even had his law office swept for bugs.

Even with this, Gary Cooper never shows, and the Board accedes to the mayor's request for another week to try and negotiate a solution with Bromell. He still doesn't get it, coming out with a public refusal to back down and end the fund-raising debacle that same day.

At a regular city council meeting held the next day, January 27, Anne Johnston demands Council order the Board to act. City council, in an extraordinary vote of unanimity, instructs the Police Services Board to call an emergency meeting and have Board lawyers seek an injunction to put an end to Operation True Blue. City council also states that any councillor who feels the need may have his or her office swept for bugs.

The Services Board meets and passes a bylaw barring political fundraising, as well as instructing its lawyers to go after an injunction in the courts. Chief Boothby enters the fray, saying he will pursue charges of discreditable conduct against the executive of the Association for not obeying his order to end Operation True Blue.

The Police Association executive issues a couple of communiqués to the public over the next few days, clearly demonstrating its intent to fight. One ad reads as follows:

> OPERATION TRUE BLUE
> THE TORONTO POLICE
> ASSOCIATION RESPONSE
>
> Much has been written and said in the past week about the efforts of the Board of Directors of the Toronto Police Association to raise funds through its

telesales project known as "Operation True Blue." It is time for the Police Association to respond.

The project is perfectly legal. The Police Services Act specifically permits the Toronto Police Association to raise funds through telesales. Section 3 of Ontario Regulation 123/98 states, in part, "A police officer does not commit misconduct [by soliciting funds] if he or she engages in the described activity in his or her capacity as an authorized representative of an association. . . ."

The media response to our campaign has been largely hysterical and based on false and misleading reports of our intentions. We have been accused of attempting to undermine democratic principles, in particular the "bullying" and "intimidating" of public officials. None of these accusations is true.

We commenced this project in an effort to make our community a safer and better place to live. Our purpose in raising funds was and is to bring about legislative change to the Young Offenders Act and the Criminal Code, and to assist in the creation of a nationwide DNA bank to enable law enforcement agencies to apprehend dangerous criminals. In addition, we intend to employ these funds to participate in the electoral process by supporting public officials who agree with these objectives.

Regardless of any past comments, it should be

noted that the funds will NOT be used to interfere with the privacy of anyone. [Author's note: This sentence was emphasized in the ad.]

We believe these goals are worthwhile and enjoy the support of a large segment of our community. It is our intention to reach every home and business within the city of Toronto. We further believe that our project constitutes a legitimate exercise of our constitutional right to be heard on matters of public importance. We reject any effort on the part of the critics to deny us our rightful place in this crucial public debate.

THE BOARD OF DIRECTORS OF THE
TORONTO POLICE ASSOCIATION

(*The Toronto Star*, 30 January 2000, p. A5.)

Three days later, the following ad appeared:

OPERATION TRUE BLUE

OPEN LETTER TO THE CITIZENS OF TORONTO

As you know, at approximately 12:00 noon on Friday, January 28, 2000, the Toronto Police Services Board passed a By-law aimed at stopping the Toronto Police Association's ("Association") Operation True Blue campaign.

Within four hours of the passing of the By-law, Chief Boothby delivered a notice to the Association ordering the Association to immediately discontinue this campaign. We believe that the By-law passed by the Police Services Board is illegal for the following reasons:

1. The Police Services Board does not have the power to regulate misconduct, only the Provincial Cabinet can do so.
2. The Regulations passed under the Police Services Act permit the Association to solicit funds. Therefore, the By-law is inconsistent with the Regulations and in effect, is an attempt by the Board to overrule the Provincial Cabinet
3. The Police Services Board does not have authority over the Association or its Board of Directors; this relationship is governed by the Collective Agreement. In addition, any Police Association which was required to act under the direction of the Chief would not be independent to act in the best interest of its members. Like any Union or Association recognized in law we are entitled to this fundamental right.
4. The By-law was passed by the Police Services Board behind closed doors and without notice as required by law.
5. The By-law violates the rights of the Association and its members to freedom of association and expression, which are fundamental freedoms guaranteed under the Charter of Rights and Freedoms.

For all these reasons, we believe that the By-law is illegal. Yet, within four hours after it was passed,

Police Chief Boothby ordered the Toronto Police Association to stop the True Blue campaign and the Police Services Board threatened to bring a court injunction to enforce that order.

There has been a lot of confusion and misunderstanding about the True Blue campaign. These concerns are unfounded. Our first concern is that the citizens of Toronto have faith in the integrity of its police officers. Secondly, President Craig Bromell is on record stating, "We are not using investigators to target politicians nor have we invaded anyone's privacy by planting bugging devices."

Operation True Blue will continue under the following guidelines in which the alterations are items three and four:

1. Telesales will continue to be conducted by an independent professional and reputable telesales company.
2. No police officers will be involved in telesales.
3. The names of persons called and whether or not they donate will not be communicated to the Toronto Police Association.
4. To address any possible misconceptions concerning the True Blue campaign, decals will no longer be part of the campaign.
5. The funds raised through the True Blue campaign will only be used for political activity permitted by the Police Services Act and its Regulations. We reiterate, the funds were never

intended and will not be used to interfere with anyone's privacy.

We believe that these features of the True Blue campaign, many of which were already in place, address any concerns members of the public may have regarding the integrity of the True Blue campaign.

Having said that, we still have to deal with the By-law and the violation of our legal rights. Although we were only given four hours notice to comply with this By-law, we gave the Police Services Board 48 hours to rescind the By-law. The Police Services Board chose not to rescind the By-law, therefore, we have served notice on both the Chief of Police and the Police Services Board that we are proceeding to court to quash their By-law and to seek significant damages for the violation of our members' rights.

The Toronto Police Association represents 7,000 members who risk their lives daily to protect members of the public in this city. Our members are committed to upholding the law. The real story here is that Chief Boothby has ordered our Executive Board to face charges even after we have complied with an illegal By-law. Secondly, the Police Services Board, which is charged with upholding the law, has passed a By-law that is, in our view, clearly illegal and which infringes upon our rights.

THE BOARD OF DIRECTORS OF THE TORONTO POLICE ASSOCIATION

(*The Toronto Star*, 2 February 2000, p. A17.)

We learn later that the Association has even fewer business smarts than it does public-relations skills. Their agreement with the telemarketing firm was outrageous in and of itself, with the Association keeping 20 percent of funds raised to the firm's 80 percent—of $306,019 pledged, only $81,820 was actually collected, and the union ended up with $16,364. It seems to be an incredibly bad deal, the worst since Esau sold his birthright for a bowl of stew.

On February 3, the union ended its fundraising drive.

Ken Higgins understands some of the frustrations, if not the tactics. "We can't have the police involved in a coercive effort to muzzle free speech. You'd never guess that we have the best justice system, the best policing in the world if you listened to the complaints, the rhetoric that's allowed to go on from citizens. I was listening to one of our phone-in shows the other day, and people were calling in and complaining about liquor seizures police made as people were disembarking from the SkyTrain. People were given free rein to make odious comparisons to Nazis, and the media lap it up; it's totally over the line.

"Nobody says, 'What have the Nazis got to do with what we're talking about?' Nobody pulls those who make those extreme statements back into line. It's like what would happen in London when I was starting out, if there was a shooting, an editor wouldn't send a reporter to the scene of the crime; he'd tell the guy to find the mother of the dead man—go for the emotion, go for the tears. Get opinions that are as far apart as possible. Whip up public anger."

Associations from police forces such as Christine Silverberg's in Calgary expressed interest in the fund-raising activities of Toronto's Finest.

COURAGE AND COSTS

"Do what you feel is right"

For anyone on the force who may disagree with the tactics or intent of the Association, watching the action for the last number of weeks would not inspire public opposition. Police who may well show great courage everyday when patrolling the city lose that courage when it comes to their own. And those police who aren't the best to begin with may well feel emboldened and protected by all the investigators and lawyers the Association keeps on retainer. Untouchable.

Deputy Chief Bob Kerr's remarkable—and costly—moment of truth on the *Fifth Estate* showed Council, and members of the Board, the effect of their refusal to deal with Bromell. While Chief Boothby is being feted across the city as his retirement day looms, Kerr sits with me in his sparsely equipped downtown office (his real office is in Scarborough) at police headquarters still looking a little shell-shocked.

"It's the way I was brought up. We all make decisions in life, do what we feel is right. There's no point in looking back. It's done. Do you know I've talked to Bromell maybe a total of ten minutes in all this time? I'd never even met him before he became president of the Association. I think he dislikes anything with stripes. He's a very angry man, empowered by inaction." He believes the "brotherhood" is stronger now than ever, that the few cases where cops do come forward (to blow the whistle) brand those cops forever.

Bob Kerr is as upright as a cop can be. He believes strongly in civilian oversight and in doing what's right. It's in his bones. He believes the "protect-ourselves" mentality lowers the standards of the force.

He comes out of small-town Ontario, a place called Prescott, which had all of five thousand residents when he left for the big city. At the age of eighteen, trying to decide what to do with his life, he was looking to the American Air Force, where his brother had enlisted, or the police. He felt he needed some structure and discipline and filled out applications for both groups. The police won.

He remembers his first trip to Toronto. "I got out at Union Station, and I didn't know how to get to police headquarters. I saw a police officer and went up to him and asked. He said, 'Why do you want to go there?' I tell him I'm joining up, and he says, 'Why the hell would you want to do that?!'"

After putting in his time as a cadet, he worked downtown at 52 Division. As a kid from a small town, he was fascinated by "the hustle and bustle of the city, the nameless winos, the diversity—the gay community, the black people. In my town, if you saw a black person, he was likely to be a porter off the train."

Kerr knows prejudice and discrimination have been

around forever, inside and outside the force. He remembers driving with his partner in the squad car, just talking, and in the midst of the story he was telling, happened to mention he was Catholic. His partner immediately pulled the car over, killed the engine, and said very seriously, "If you want to get anywhere in this department, don't go around telling people you're Catholic."

Toronto police were then overwhelmingly white, male Anglo-Saxons, drawn primarily from Irish, Scottish, and English families. And cops were uniformly big men, "brawn was used a lot more then," and Kerr was small—at five foot, eleven inches—for the times. He remembers the Portuguese and Italian communities had concerns back then, very similar to those expressed by other immigrant groups now; he remembers demonstrations and flare-ups over the death of a young Portuguese man shot and killed by police.

Kerr believes, "If you treat people with respect, fairly and within the law, you won't have a problem. Don't judge people by their appearance or by your value system." He believes police were much better diplomats when they patrolled in one-person cars—out of sheer necessity and self-interest. "You learned to be a diplomat pretty quickly. We lost a certain amount of that when we went to two officers in a car."

There is also a loss when two officers walk a beat as opposed to one patrolman, the cops tend to talk to each other more than they do to members of the community. He knows how terrible the force is about getting the "few bad apples" out, and it infuriates him that the paramilitary internal disciplinary system doesn't allow the immediate, same-day firing, that the labour law would permit at General Motors.

"We can't even suspend without pay. The optics of an officer charged with sexual assault or even armed robbery sitting at home getting a paycheque are terrible."

I looked across the desk at this honourable man, and said, "I know you said that you weren't the leak."

"I wasn't."

"I know. But whoever blew the whistle—they did the right thing."

His head is down, listening and thinking. Then, almost too quietly to hear, he says, staring intently at me, "That's what I should have said. That even though it wasn't me, it was the right thing to do."

He will be handing in his papers in March; that had been his intention before the threats and media storms.

I'm so angry over the next few weeks: a decent man looking back over the wreckage of a career of public service, a man who believes in doing the right thing, essentially betrayed by the inability, the unwillingness of politicians and his superiors, to help him draw the line.

As I'm writing this, Elian Gonzalez has been taken out of the home of his Miami relatives by armed officers. The three-month saga of moral bankruptcy displayed by everyone involved, terrified of the electoral consequences of upsetting the Cuban refugee community, is the same kind of thing writ large.

In some of her speeches, Christine Silverberg tells about

the work of Richard Ayres (at the Center for Labor Management Studies in the United States) who has developed a template for measuring an agency's sensitivity to ethical conduct. His paper was released in 1988 by the FBI at the Major Cities Chiefs Round Table.

- Does your police department have a simple, easily understood statement of values that is known throughout and embodies the fundamental notions of ethical behaviour and principled decision-making in how we approach our work, manage internally and relate to the community?
- Does your agency's leadership consistently and personally communicate the organization's core beliefs throughout the workplace and the community to reinforce Service ethic and build respect in the community?
- Has your police agency articulated a clear picture of desirable, undesirable, and unacceptable behaviours by initiating ethics training for all employees to ensure that they understand the importance of doing the right thing and making the right decision based on the organization's core beliefs?
- Does your department have an open, formal system and structure to encourage and receive all citizens' complaints?
- Does your Service have stringent recruitment and background investigation procedures to ensure that only those individuals exhibiting the highest ethical standards and qualifications are hired?

- Does the community's impression and assessment of your police officers include characterizations such as professional, honest, sense of integrity, fair, courageous, service-oriented and respect for the individual?
- Does your police agency depend on close supervision and extravagant control procedures to get the job done, or does it rely on the organization's core beliefs and employee character, expecting employees to do what is right because it's the right thing to do?
- Has your police force established clear guidelines around conflict of interest in regards to secondary employment?
- Does your police force consistently take strong disciplinary sanctions against employees who violate the Service's values regardless of position and rank?
- Are your supervisors and managers held accountable for monitoring their employees' compliance with regulations, policies, and organizational values, and when necessary, taking appropriate action to correct deficiencies, counsel, coach and/or report misconduct?
- Does your police department's performance appraisal contain questions that pertain to demonstrated attitudes and behaviours that support the Service's core values?
- Do citizens trust your police department to maintain proper discipline and thoroughly investigate allegations of corruption or police misconduct?
- Has your police agency created an environment that sustains and reinforces good behaviour by rewarding

employees who consistently demonstrate the organization's values?

- Is your police department free from political interference as it pertains to promotions, assignments, and operational priorities?

To many of these points, I believe we would have to answer "no," on the basis of what we've seen.

Chief Fantino was almost anointed by the Province. At least one Police Services Board member complained about "undue haste" in the decision-making. While Mission and Value statements look good, and may help some citizens feel easier about their police force, no one seems to be dealing with the parallel—and more widely accepted—subterranean values of cover-up, silence, and tolerance of negative behaviours.

Popular opinion has it that Fantino was hired in order to offset the Police Association, that the Board wanted someone tougher than Bromell to keep him in line.

Communities and Crime

TAKING IT TO THE STREET

"Nobody knows the troubles I've seen"

It can be as difficult to live in a "high crime" area as it is to police it. Communities that constantly find themselves in the media because of over-reported shootings or drug busts or assaults tend to lose hope that change for the better is possible.

Poverty often dictates geography: People go where the rents are cheap, where landlords won't turn you away because you're on social assistance, since that is the income source of the majority of their tenants—single mothers with limited options, new immigrants, the unemployed, the undereducated, crammed into ill-kept buildings, either privately owned or in huge public-housing developments.

Where there is despair, there are those who will profit from it: slum landlords, young men and women who sell a variety of drugs, others who break into homes or mug their neighbours or sell their bodies in order to pay for them.

No one wants to live in fear.

In communities such as Regent Park and Jane-Finch in Toronto, or Downtown Eastside in Vancouver, good people learn that minding your own business is the key to survival. Ratting out the local drug dealer has lethal consequences. Responding to a woman's screams across the hall might bring the batterer to your door.

The fear of losing a child, a teenager, to a stray bullet in a drug deal gone bad is stronger for many than the fear of what the police might do to that same child if they stop and question him.

It's possible to teach children how to handle cops without aggravating the situation; it's a lot harder to deal with the consequences of being in the wrong place at the wrong time.

Residents of poor communities are no more tolerant of crime than they are anywhere else—they would love to see a heavier police presence; they would love to feel safe in their own homes. There is a real frustration when it seems nothing is being done, crime continues unabated, and "there's never a cop when you need one."

That frustration can go over the top when, instead of targeting the criminal element, the police instead appear to harass the innocent, the young—effectively seeming to tar everyone with the same brush.

In Toronto, 51 Division has been christened by the cops who work out of it as Fort Apache, and it's also known as the punishment division. This can't be too encouraging for the residents of the communities served by the men and women of 51 Division, like Regent Park.

It's one of life's little oddities that the things the community and the police say about each other—what they complain about—in Regent Park, are interchangeable and, if you took away the attribution of "police officer" or "resident," indistinguishable.

When Jim Ward, a Toronto consultant, was commissioned by the Police Services Board in 1996 to do a report on policing issues in Regent Park, he worked with a group of three cops from 51 Division and three community residents.

> The police perceive Regent Park as a densely populated, ethnically diverse, low-income area that is difficult to police because of the physical layout and insufficient community support for their efforts. In addition, it is seen as a community with a long history of poor police-community relations and one where media-exacerbated stigma makes positive initiatives difficult. (*Police-Community Issues in Regent Park*, by Jim Ward, 1996, p. 62.)
>
> Most residents see the mass media as portraying Regent Park in a negative light and as worsening local police-community relations. For some residents the physical layout of Regent Park, with its many dead-ended streets and blind alleyways constitutes a safety problem. . . . Residents would like

> to see a greater police presence and a tougher approach to criminals who operate in the community. They would also like to see greater respect towards them, and for the police to get to know the community more thoroughly.
>
> Drugs, prostitution, violence and break-and-entry constitute the major crime problems for residents. Child safety and racism constitute the major safety problems." (Jim Ward's report, p. 29.)

> Police work in Regent Park is challenging and rewarding in terms of variety. It is a location offering a broad range of policing experience. Successful drug arrests, prostitute and john suppression, increasing communication with children and proactive policing are seen to be the most effective aspects of the work. Negative aspects . . . include: being accused of being racist; lack of community respect, presence of weapons, difficulty in distinguishing the "bad guys" from the "good guys," the difficulty in keeping criminals out of action for long; the attractiveness of Regent Park to drug dealers, both those who are local residents and outsiders; the lack of community support. (Jim Ward's report, p. 62.)

Local residents seem to be saying, amongst other things, that they don't want to be treated like a criminal simply because of their address, and the cops similarly don't want to be treated like racists just because they're cops.

Cops worry about their own safety when making arrests. This fear seems to be based on the possibility of being surrounded by angry citizens—there are too few police and too many guns. Residents say they would like to see "a greater police presence in the well-known 'hot spots' in the community. They would also appreciate more police presence inside the high-rise buildings."

When Jim Ward was interviewing police for his project, he noticed on the bulletin boards of 51 Division an advisory to officers from their Association representative not to participate in the study, although, aside from general conspiracy theories, he couldn't tell why.

He believes the advisory was posted by Police Association President Craig Bromell, who was then assigned to 51 Division. Bromell had already made his bones as a union representative in 51, taking on the police hierarchy with a shutdown of the Division. I can understand the reluctance to participate, the fear that it would result only in more blame being put on the cops.

During one of my last nights as a worker at PARC, I was attending to a man who lived on the street and pretty much drank anything that could give him a buzz. He hung out with a crowd of fellow travellers, and the threat of violence was common, centering around ownership of a bottle of wine or tube of glue. This man had collapsed in an alcove next to the Centre, his face was horribly battered, his eye so swollen and bloody, I feared it would simply fall on the pavement. He kept holding his side, so the possibility of cracked ribs was also quite real.

I knew that it was simply his turn to be the target of his peers. I also knew he had participated in beating up others. Still, as I sat with him on the cold pavement, wiping vomit off his face, trying to calm his fears that his friends would come back, and dealing with the angry looks and resentments of passers-by, the futility of trying to help him, when there was really nowhere for him to go and no one wanted him, got to me. The police had refused to come out, saying he'd already been taken to the hospital and walked out before being examined and after stealing a large bottle of rubbing alcohol.

He was taking swigs from that bottle, now all bloody, as we huddled together. He told me about his home in the Maritimes, about the parents he once had. A helper and I used the fact of his drinking to suggest he was now in a dangerous, toxic state, to get the ambulance and police to attend.

The cops were angry when they arrived, all three of them wearing rubber gloves, coming up to where my friend now slumped unconscious. One cop took the lead, reaching down and grabbing the man by the hair, lifting up his head.

Immediately, all my frustration and anger and despair had a target: "What the hell are you doing? Leave him alone!"

The cop jumped back, looking at his fellow officers in a defensive "I didn't touch him, what are you talking about" way.

And we had a face-off there on the street, confirming for the cop that community workers are cop bashers, confirming for me—in that instance—the insensitivity of the police. I got the PARC members to help lift the victim towards the ambulance, treating him as a man and not as garbage.

DOWNTOWN EASTSIDE
"Pain and Wasting"

The invitation came in the mail, a gray card with a picture of two police officers videotaping a very thin woman in a graffiti-filled alleyway. Inside the card, a white insert announced:

> The National Film Board of Canada, in association with the Vancouver Police Department and CBC television, invites you to the world premiere of *Through a Blue Lens*, directed by Veronica Alice Mannix.
>
> The Vancouver Police Pipe Band and the Vancouver Police Ceremonial Marching Unit will introduce the program.
>
> The streets of Vancouver's Downtown Eastside, home to Canada's worst drug and HIV crisis, are also the setting for an innovative police initiative. Armed with video cameras, seven officers—called the Odd Squad—walk the beat recording the lives of addicts, and bring the images and stories they gather together to high school students. *Through a Blue Lens* puts a human face to the world of drug addiction as we follow the lives of six addicts and their

> relationships with the seven officers over the period of one year.
>
> Watch for "Through a Blue Lens," an upcoming CBC special on *The Magazine.*

I couldn't go to the première, but I asked Toby Hinton and Al Arsenault to send me the invitation anyway. It was difficult not to feel a part of the project and the excitement just coming to fruition over the year we'd talked together.

I've seen few places in Canada more resistant to positive change than the Downtown Eastside (DES), even fewer where men and women have been so reduced by addiction and its consequences as to—at times—challenge any remaining belief in their humanity. It's a neighbourhood that easily breeds and confirms cynicism and anger in those who police it, where life is indistinguishable from a walking, crawling, gray death. Drugs are everywhere—cocaine, heroin, crack, morphine—all you need is the money to buy them. Toby Hinton calls the corner of East Hastings and Main "Pain and Wasting." When talking with him, I find myself wishing that all cops were as thoughtful and compassionate.

The cops get criticized for doing their jobs, for not doing their jobs, for busting people and not busting people, for their presence and for their absence. The cops patrol, walking their beat through the desolate streets, peering down alleyways, moving people along; they loom large in their uniforms, unnaturally healthy in the dead zone, unnaturally clean among the homeless.

And it never gets any better. Lock up one dealer, ten

more spring up to take his place for the little time the courts will hand him. A constant supply of young people drift in, from other parts of the city, from other parts of the country. But wherever they come from, whatever background, class, or education they bring with them, a few months in the DES and they find themselves trapped, unable to leave.

I am still haunted by memories of the collapsed bodies in filthy alleyways, the broken, discarded, disease-ridden men and women who live only for the next hit, who sometimes will kill one another for the price of a high.

The average Vancouver citizen seems to accept that what happens to the addicts in the DES can't be fixed, so the area has attained a kind of weird normality in the city. However, what addicts do to themselves is one thing, but how they get the money to pay for the drugs is quite another. Crimes against property, businesses, or outside individuals are never met with that *laissez-faire* attitude, but "We want something done about this, and we want it done immediately."

Nice neighbourhoods border the DES, with working- and middle-class citizens living in single-family homes and eating in clean restaurants and shopping in upscale places. People from nice neighbourhoods pressure the police to clean up the streets and alleyways, get rid of the prostitutes and the break-and-enter criminals and the discarded condoms and needles.

I wondered about the cops, too, as I stood surrounded by dealers and buyers in a narcotic free-for-all across the street from the police station. Why weren't they doing something? The better question would be: Why should we expect them to be any more proactive or successful than the litany of failed agency interventions, failed government drug policies, failed activists' organizations?

But for many frustrated people, who just want the problem gone, or at least driven out of sight, it's the police failure that rankles the most. Pressure is increased on politicians, who pressure the police, who bang heads on the streets.

Ken Higgins, who is passionate about policing, attended a recent meeting in Vancouver where the solution proposed by a group of activists was to declare a "free zone" in the DES, where police could not enter. A kind of mini-Amsterdam where anything goes.

He sighed with frustration over the phone: "It's just not on. The DES has always been a challenge, a political hot potato."

In 1984, having spent some time as the executive assistant to the chief of police, he was made an inspector, and the challenge was his. His immediate predecessor in the area had instituted monthly meetings with representatives of various agencies working in the area (the Carnegie Centre, the Downtown Eastside Residents Association, youth groups, and involved churches), and he saw this as sensible and worth continuing. Providers in the area had a right to know what the police were up to and the right to tell him what they saw as issues or trends. There was a separate process to deal with individual complaints, so as not to derail discussions.

"If I was getting a lot of complaints about hookers in a particular area, I could let those who work with the women know, and they would ask the women to avoid that place for a while."

He'd go out with a sergeant or staff sergeant to visit the hot spots. Even as a constable he knew he had to "get to know people, get out of the patrol car: bartenders, waiters, variety-store owners—better observers of what's going on. It's essential to have the kind of relationship, where you can talk about a whole bunch of innocuous things, so that when the time comes, when you need real information, they're not frightened to tell you."

Along with drugs, the DES always has the highest consumption of beer per seat in bars. "We know through the liquor commission how much is ordered, so if there's 160 seats in a bar, you just divide those by how many gallons was ordered." Laughing a little sadly, Ken adds that this poor community seems to have a huge number of gourmet cooks if one goes by the sale of rice wine and cooking wine.

Although he's been retired for eighteen months, he's still in touch with some of the people he worked with in the DES. "Things still don't seem to change along the lines people profess to be working towards.

"You don't have to have a degree in sociology to know it's not working. The mentality that pervades here is 'people get what they deserve.' Everyone is tarred with that same brush, including people who just try to eke out a small living in an SRO (single-room occupancy hotel), people who don't abuse welfare, don't deal drugs—if they're in the neighbourhood, they've got to be criminals. If you believe that people are fundamentally worthwhile, if we claim to be a caring, value-driven society, you can't ever get to the point where you pull the pin, leave them to self-destruct.

"Drugs are a country-wide problem. Even if, to counteract NIMBY (not in my back yard) the government declared: 'There shall be rehab houses in every community'; if we didn't add a single addict to our numbers, it would still take years and years of effort to rehabilitate those who've been left to deal with injection drug use on their own."

Ken is not in favour of legalizing drugs and worries about the current push to legalize pot. "People, including parents, who feel that the occasional joint they smoked in college [and by the way, he never did] was no big deal and did them no harm, don't understand that it's not the same dope. That now it's like their kids, or someone else's, smoking eight or nine joints of the 'wacky weed' of the sixties. We'd make a huge mistake legalizing pot without a thorough evaluation. Is it a road to addiction to harder drugs?"

COPS AND CAMERAS

"There are so many Kodak moments"

Al Arsenault doesn't see the de-criminalization of pot as the beginning of a drug Armageddon. Al is compact and muscular; he's colourful, a born talker. "You don't see addicts committing armed robbery to buy pot. And if two pot heads are fighting, it's more likely to result in giggles than stabbings. On the other hand, if a twelve-year-old wants to get a buzz on, and in order to do that he has to get his hands on a six-pack of beer, it's quite a time-consuming process. With pot, however, it just takes a few tokes—no muss, no fuss—and he's off to the races. Then he might say, 'I'll smoke a joint after my homework,' then that becomes, 'I'll smoke before doing my homework,' and finally, 'To hell with homework.' I worry about kids losing their motivation early in life."

He's pretty scornful about the so-called "war on drugs" declarations. "A war means the whole country's behind it, and that's simply not the case. If you don't have the citizenry behind you, then it becomes like a military acting without public support, like Vietnam, an unwinnable situation. There's more of a war on drunk driving than on drugs, and that seems to be working. Thirty years ago, if someone told you they got smashed and then drove home, you might have laughed; now you look at the guy like 'what an asshole.'"

Al's honest, even blunt about his work and his attitudes, and you might assume he'd be a hard-ass kind of street cop, cynical, indifferent to the suffering around him, putting in his time and collecting his pay. It happens. But not to him. This is a cop who's been reborn, who's displaying all the enthusiasm and caring of an idealistic rookie, and it's all due to a serendipitous meeting with an other officer, Toby Hinton.

It was at a Beat Cops beer-bash reunion, held in the

basement of a local SRO—a gathering of all those cops who'd walked a beat in the DES. Al carried a camera around with him, a habit he'd picked up when "I'd spent nine months working for Bell, climbing poles, and after I finished I really regretted that I had no pictures of me in all my gear. And on the beat, there are so many Kodak moments."

He'd converted some of his snaps of the characters he'd encountered on the job to slides, and as the party got rolling, he showed them to the assembled cops. It was a big hit, triggering stories and memories. Toby Hinton was especially interested; he guest-lectured every now and then at his wife's forensic university classes, and he knew how valuable the slides would be as a learning aid for the students.

Toby had ten years on the force to Al's twenty. Both have degrees; Al holds a B.Sc. and and a B.Ed., Toby a B.A. in Political Science and Criminology. They both wanted to make a difference in drug education and prevention, stop the influx of young people into the DES.

The Odd Squad was created when, together with five other constables, they pooled their own money to buy a broadcast-quality video camera and started carrying that camera on their beat. (Filmmaker Veronica Mannix and her cameraman husband, Daniel Mannix, happened to be completing their own documentary in the DES when she ran into the members of the Odd Squad, and they eventually teamed up.)

Neither of these guys are any more enamoured of the system they work within than Craig Bromell is. And the

Downtown Eastside makes Toronto's Regent Park look like a walk in the park.

Al especially seems to be in a constant battle with his supervisors. This dynamic duo had called to give me a heads-up that they were going to be on *The Vicki Gabereau Show* on CTV the next day, promoting the film. They came on right after Isabel Allende, who was pushing her new book. They were both in uniform, and looked pretty sharp; but both carried their street personas with them.

At one point, Vicki, who seemed to be enjoying them enormously, leaned closer to Al, peered intently at him, then asked with disbelief in her voice: "Is that an earring?"

Toby answered for his partner: "He's just baiting them, just waiting for someone to come after him."

Al tells me later that it is indeed a kind of baiting. "One of my sergeants is a lesbian, a great lady, and she wears one earring. I keep checking in with her, telling her to keep it in, 'cause I'm going to claim there's a double standard at work if they tell me to lose mine. If all else fails, I'll say it's part of my religion, you know, a representation of the yin and yang sign."

He also tells me that Vicki had a great coughing fit before the shoot, a good five minutes, and that when he signed her guest book, he wrote, "Thanks for not coughing up a lung on me."

It's easy to see how close these two guys are, how attuned to each other, and how ready with a fast remark. That peculiar quality of street toughness is shot through with a very non-traditional empathy and hope.

DRUGS, FILMS, AND HOPE

"Chasing that feeling"

When Al goes into high schools these days, he doesn't preach at them, and he believes the kids appreciate that fact. "I tell kids that smack is like the best orgasm you'll ever have, times ten. Probably the best feeling you'll have in your whole life. But you'll chase that feeling again and again, and long after your brain has kicked in, said it's time to stop, your body will still be wanting it. Your body can't turn off the urge for it."

He likes to use a "sandwich" analogy: "I ask them if they were stopped on the street by a stranger offering them a sandwich, wrapped in plastic, would they take it? 'No,' they say, like it's a dumb question. So then I say, 'What if the guy is dressed really nicely, drives a great car, would you take it then?' 'No,' they'll tell me. 'And what if you knew that that sandwich had gone through the hands of four very hungry people, each of whom took out a bit of the meat and stuck in some filler, so no one would notice, would you take it?' 'No,' 'no,' and 'no' they'll say. So, what do you think you're putting in your body when you buy off the street, how many times—and with what—has it been stepped on, as hungry addicts take their cut and put God-knows-what in its stead? Strychnine?'"

He believes "We've got to look at the community taking responsibility. Police get a call at three in the morning: 'What are you gonna do about my kid who isn't home yet.' What can we do? We're just the people waving little sticks around."

But they can and do make a difference.

Al told me about a dramatic impact the Odd Squad made: "The DES has been trying for years to get rice wine, cooking wine, taken off the shelves of grocery stores and put into liquor stores instead. There was no movement. I was asked by one of my sergeants, 'Do you have any video involving the problems associated with rice wine?' and I said 'No, but we could make some.'

"The government and the public mostly get statistics, and they move no one. We went out and put faces to the stats. We got this dead guy's brother, the dead guy is lying on a SRO bed, to talk about how his brother wasted away on this stuff, the coroner saying how it can turn the guts of a four-year-old into those of an eighty-year-old, and a couple of droolers whose brains are so fried from that shit that they barely make sense—powerful imagery! And just like that, you know, five minutes after parts of the video played on the news, the attorney general is taking action.

"So who's unhappy?

"This woman who leads a rice-wine users' group, she's saying we didn't get people's consent, but we did—except for the dead guy, but his brother consented—and why are they against us? Just because it was police who got it done."

I have a lot of time for Toby and Al. I believe what I feel towards them is gratitude, plain and simple—for doing something, for trying to help. If you've ever met a mother who's travelled across the country to wander the streets of the DES looking for a lost son or daughter, if you have a friend or relative enslaved by crack or dying of AIDS from injecting with dirty needles, you'll probably feel the same way.

Al and Toby could have lost themselves in burn-out and resentment, directed towards the force, community activists, or those they police, said screw it, who needs it; instead they grew more committed to education, prevention, and communication.

The opening shot of the documentary "Through a Blue Lens" shows the corner of East Hastings and Main. I remember the feel of the place, the buying and selling going on at the foot of the steps of the Carnegie Centre. The smell, the feel of grit at the back of your throat.

The camera moves to Toby and Al, in uniform, standing at the entrance of an alley. Toby says every now and then they go through it "like a blue tide." They stop to talk to a figure huddled in an alcove. He doesn't respond; they realize he's overdosed. They call an ambulance—he's stopped breathing. A flurry of activity, oxygen forced into his lungs, a full five minutes later he starts to come around, "What's going on?" he asks, still groggy. Either Toby or Al can be heard saying: "You're back from the dead, sir."

He did more drugs that night and for another six months.

Toby says he used to be a lot more hard-nosed when he got out of the academy; now, he says, he's turned into a softy.

Al's standing in front of a high-school class; he's showing the kids a picture of Shannon. He'd asked her when she first arrived in the DES if he could take photos of her. She's eighteen, fresh-faced, dressed like the students in the class. It was taken at midnight, and she's standing in front of a bar where she'd been drinking and looking for drugs.

He asks the kids: "Is this an addict?"

Everyone says, "No."

"What's an addict look like?"

"A bum. Dirty."

The next photo of her was taken six months later. You can hear the sharp intake of breath, see the shock on their faces. Some of them look like they want to cry. It's a radical transformation, but six months of doing cocaine and heroin can do that to you.

Carmelita (Carlee) has recently lost her boyfriend. He'd been trying to clean himself up, but couldn't deal with the need. He blew his head off in front of her. She's trying to cope. Her arm is swollen and infected, a horrible seeping gash. She keeps trying to pull bugs out of her arm. Another member of the Odd Squad asks if she'd mind being filmed, explaining that it's to discourage kids from showing up in the area. She thinks for a moment, then says "Yeah, yeah, I'll do that."

Nikki's been an addict for twenty-five years. Sitting on the pavement on a pile of rags, she greets the two beat cops like old friends. She's street tough, profane, and a wreck: That she's even alive is a miracle. It's hard to tell from how she looks, but she comes from a good, middle-class family.

Toby tells me how Nikki "lived in alleyways and things, and one night behind the Regent Hotel she set fire to a whole pile of shit, the owners kicked up a ruckus because they'd have to clean it up. I asked her why she'd done it and she gave me two reasons: 'It purifies the soul, and besides, it's the only way to get the smell of shit from the alley.'"

She'd asked Toby to try and find her a tent. She kept bugging him so he'd said he'd keep an eye out. Before he could find one, he found her in the heart of the skids, in a vacant lot right beside a broken washing machine, all set up in this really nice tent.

With her permission, they'd used her picture in some of the promos, showing it to some of the local business people. Toby adds: "The owner of the bar—he's a member of BarWatch; he'd even donated a little money to the project—he starts shouting, 'Hey, where'd she get the tent, that's my fucking tent, there's that stain on the door flap!' Turns out his cleaner had put it out to air, and Nikki, of course, thinking it was thrown out, scooped it."

To the Odd Squad, the night of the launch was pure magic. Toby tells me, "We couldn't have asked for better. There were more than 1,200 people there, from all walks of life—judges, lawyers, people from the different community groups, ex-addicts, doctors—it was unbelievable. And no one complained! Usually someone's going to complain, saying it's exploitation or crass, whatever, 'cause it's cops, but nothing but accolades. Even from the chain of command. We've had calls from A&E, *20/20*, German television, the *New York Times*! Almost 500 people jammed into the reception after."

In the film, Nikki had wondered if there was money to buy a new dress so she'd look okay for the opening. And after the film ended, Nikki got up on stage, and started off by saying: "I guess you can see I got my dress." She thanked the Odd Squad for what they'd done for her and what they'd done to keep kids from ending up on the street. The crowd gave her a standing ovation.

After "Through a Blue Lens" aired on CBC's *The Magazine*, it was followed by a discussion with experts, and Nikki was one of those experts. The transition from the street wraith to this articulate woman hasn't been easy; twenty-five years of her life in the skids have left her haunted and fearful that this may all be a dream and that she'll wake up huddled in an alleyway. She's back with her very supportive family and attending rehab.

Randy, a former all-star athlete, was considered one of the "most extreme addicts" in the DES. In the documentary, he's shown muttering to himself, flailing around in a kind of seizure, with wildly tangled beard and hair, looking ancient. Nothing like the quiet, clean-shaven, nicely dressed young man who watches himself on the screen in a kind of horror, saying, "I thought I was having fun."

He's been clean for over a year.

The same story is repeated with five of the six profiled in the documentary. That is a better success rate than most professionals and agencies can claim, and it started with a couple of cops talking to street addicts, asking for their help to keep kids away from the life, and getting to know these discarded people—as people.

Al's casting around about what to do next. He's come up with a Save One Soul movement.

"We wouldn't go out and say, 'There's five hundred people we're raising money for.' We may have to leave 499 to rot—they're going to anyway—and concentrate all our resources on the one person, whoever that may be. We'll have to work that out. But we think the first person will be one of the people in our video. We'll raise enough money, say $40,000, to hire one person to spend all his time with this addict, helping him clean up, connecting him to housing and work. If the person is interested, say, in veterinary medicine, go to an animal clinic and ask if there's sweeping-up to do, just so the guy can get real exposure, maybe work their way up. Then, when that guy or woman is settled, move on to the next person."

To Al, there's the four H's: Habit elimination; mental, spiritual, and emotional Health; affordable, safe Housing; and Hope creation. A better mission statement I've yet to see.

COMMUNITY POLICING

"Flipping hamburgers"

Ken Higgins likes to repeat something he heard, which struck a chord, from a proponent of community policing: "When people say they're going fishing, they don't say, I'm going fishing for fish. It's implicit. In the same way, we shouldn't have to say community policing, there's a redundancy there."

Jeff McArthur knows that the nature of policing is changing and that he must change with it. But he's so wistful when he tries to explain, even about the new restrictions around high-speed chases: "They have a lot more restrictions now, but I've got to say, it was an awful lot of fun. I know I shouldn't say that, but, you know, dentists try to prevent tooth decay, and that's probably satisfying, but I bet they're happier if they get a really exciting problem to solve. You live for the big armed robbery."

To Toronto's Mike Boyd, who was in at the beginning as Chief Boothby moved the whole organization to community policing "one month and eighteen days after he became chief," resistance to the new direction arose out of a misunderstanding of what it meant: "Though there's fewer today than two and a half years ago, or four and a half years ago, who don't get it. We need to explain to them that community policing does mean making arrests and fighting crime. In the old system, we had Community Relations Units, officers who could go out and speak with organizations and community people. But those same people would say, 'These aren't the police we have a problem with. These aren't the ones who arrest people or come around to investigate break-and-enters.' And it's true that the so-called 'coffee-and-cookie squad' wasn't at the time doing hard policing. They were there to shake hands, turn up at community events, what's known around the force as 'flipping hamburgers.'

"It shouldn't just be Community Relations that acts respectfully," Mike says. "I came to understand the weakness of that way of doing things. The community wants to see our police demonstrating professionalism and being mindful of community relations in their day-to-day work. They want us to help them address community problems. I personally don't buy the claim of some officers that people don't like them just because they're cops—it's how those cops behave towards the public that determines how they're viewed."

Community policing also means a new way of judging successful policing.

"It's not the number of arrests, or the number of summonses. We need to judge our work by results rather than actions. If, for instance, a community is being plagued by B&Es, and we put a half dozen officers on their streets as well as fifteen, twenty community people, you effectively scare off the bad guys, and the absence of B&Es becomes the measure of success."

The first macro community policing they did was to fight for a court diversion program for those men prowling communities looking for prostitutes.

Mike says, "We had to move away from approaching prostitution from a morals perspective, which didn't really work anyway. Members of a particular community may complain that the presence of prostitutes in the area has led to the abusive, derogatory harassment of women and children and infested public parks and laneways with used needles and condoms. We met with the attorney general and created a diversion program for johns.

"The John School Program has been in effect for three and a half years, with a total of 2,550 men attending. Thus far, only eight have been re-arrested or re-investigated for frequenting the area where they were originally arrested."

Proactive community policing can also happen on the nation's highways.

At the time of our interview, Peggy Gamble headed up a nine-member team of Highway Rangers, probably the most diverse squad around: "Two blacks, two Caucasians, one Japanese Canadian, and four women. Our police should mirror the communities they patrol. Traffic is our life. The highways are our community, and it's up to us to make them as safe as possible."

She adds that she loves cars, loves driving, and (adding that she probably shouldn't be telling me this) loves putting on the siren and racing off after bad guys. She almost glows with pride and commitment. I think she was born to protect the rest of us.

The Rangers are one of Bill Currie's initiatives. As the provincial elections were nearing around 1995, the polls showed Conservative leader Mike Harris was a real contender, and one of the promises he ran on was to remove photo-radar. Bill thought he ought to have a proposal ready, just in case Harris won, since removing photo-radar would necessitate some form of replacement deterrent.

He came up with two squads of nine officers, all with some public-relations skills—an ability to talk to people—and had members of those squads stay together to police the highways. It was impossible to miss the police presence on the roads, five to seven cars to a bunch, ranging throughout the Greater Toronto Area (GTA).

"The goal was to talk to people, to do some educating, Everyone stopped by cops like this would be certain to tell his family and friends about it—it makes a good story. And you get your message about safe driving across."

His target was 50,000 stops a year over a five-year period. By that point, a quarter of a million people would have been reached, not to mention the millions of their friends and relations. And, he's proud to say, they've never had one formal complaint lodged against them. "We used to get complaints all the time."

He's not sure if the change has come about because everyone behaves for different reasons; the guy who's been stopped may behave because there's so many cops; the cops may behave because other cops are watching.

Peggy also believes in knowing and being known in the community where you live. "Myself, I live in a fairly new sub-division in Kitchener. Everyone there is professional; the houses range from $150,000 to $200,000. It's a nice area, I know all my neighbours. I know what kinds of cars they drive and what cars don't belong. People will come and ask me if they're not sure about something, before they do it."

Driving with Peggy is an interesting experience, although I'm more used to some of the equipment by now, including the large computerized metal box between us, with all the take-down, siren, and loudspeaker buttons. Every now and then her portable phone rings—with the Lone Ranger theme.

She's not very tall, and I notice she has to work the gas and brake with a somewhat strained leg and foot. I ask why she doesn't pull the seat forward, and she explains that she likes to keep the optimum safe distance from the airbag. She's a perfectionist.

One of our meetings had to be cancelled so she could attend a special session on what she thought was a Y2K thing, but it turned out to be a session on what would be expected of the police if the nuclear reactor near Whitby got into trouble.

"They were telling us things like, everything's fine, no problems expected that we can't deal with, but in the unlikely event something did, you might have to go inside, and that radiation might be spread ten miles around the area, depending on the weather, and I said, no way. I live in Kitchener, I don't want to turn green, and I'm not going into a hot zone with no protection. If you get us some suits, TYVEK suits, okay. Otherwise you'll just have to fire me."

Bill Currie had just been promoted, and in our first meeting Peggy had some concerns about who would replace him, since there "are still some dinosaurs in the service," but now that Jay Hope is at the helm, Peggy seems content.

POLICING AND ABORIGINALS

"I talk to them about my life"

Community policing by aboriginal police services is probably the truest example of what can happen when it's done right.

Glen Bannen's office is in a 24-square-foot cedar building with a rounded front, creating the look of half a teepee, with the thirteen cedar logs holding up the front representing the thirteen full moons in a year. His office is located in the Garden River First Nations reserve, where 1,800 people live. It's a well-developed reserve, with a large Administration Centre, a Health and Community Centre, a daycare, and a large volunteer fire department. Glen seems larger than life, but he has a huge laugh and he's a determined fighter.

"We've also got construction companies, local confectioneries, and a gas bar, 'cause you know the Trans-Canada cuts right through."

In his opinion, the aboriginal police force doesn't get a lot of negative attitude about policing their communities. On the contrary, there is a lot of pride and growing trust, which is oddly proving to be a big challenge.

"The more people trust us, the more they tell us, the more they expect from us. We need to be very clear what we can and can't do. We have communities of 2,000 people with five worker bees. Government offices shut down at four o'clock; we're here twenty-four hours a day, seven days a week. If we're dealing with a sexual assault, who's looking into the welfare of the victim, and who's there to help with the accused?"

They are trying to work out a memorandum of agreement with their communities, spelling out very clearly and exactly what their role is, and they've begun meetings with caregivers and service providers to look at picking up the slack. It's interesting to think of the police as a catalyst to get responsive services for the community.

"We want to be proactive in eliminating crime, be visible in the band office and at the daycare. Spending two hours with a five-year-old will mean a savings of hundreds of hours and thousands of dollars later on when he's reached his teenage years. Right now, aboriginals make up 4 percent of the population of this country, and 65 percent of the prison population."

Karen Bell knows there is also a downside to all this closeness to the community. As a sergeant working out of the same Garden River reserve where she grew up, she has to be careful where and with whom she socializes, especially if there is liquor at a party.

"I have to be very aware of what I say, who I sit next to, what and how much I drink. Across the room is likely to be someone I once arrested, and he'll mouth off as he gets more drunk. And I know better than to attend some functions. I mostly associate with friends and family. In Toronto, there were about thirty officers on our shift, we all had shift parties, and you got to know the people you worked with. I tried to tell myself then not to just socialize with cops; on my days off, I didn't want to be talking about the job."

In a more supervisory than frontline position these days, Karen also still works with sexual assault victims and says: "I take great interest, and I'm very sensitive to females who come forward with sexual assault complaints. I know you're just supposed to go and do a job, but I've brought some anger with me. A twenty-three-year-old who's been messed up all her life just complained to me about an uncle who molested her between the ages of six and fifteen. There are a lot of kids still being abused. Sometimes it's a neighbour, when the parents are both working—and you just want to yell, 'Doesn't this man know what he's doing to this child, to this community!?' "

In the best kind of proactive community policing, Karen sometimes goes into the Sault, where some teachers are having trouble handling inner-city native children.

"The teacher will threaten to phone the parents, and the kid will say, 'So what, she's always drunk anyway.' I talk to them about my life, and why I'm a cop, and I find that they really listen and show sympathy and understanding. I tell them, 'I hope when you see me around, you won't think I'm there just to arrest people. I hope you won't hesitate to say hello.' "

We can only imagine what this kind of frankness might mean to a troubled kid who can't see any way out of her or his situation.

Command and Control

CHALLENGES AND CHANGE

"No, it would break the rules"

Today, there is considerable strain on police officers. They are portrayed as professionals, yet simultaneously, within their organizations, within their governing framework, they are often treated as children, not mature adults. At its worst, the end result is that vital police officer discretion is driven underground and the creativity and productivity of police officers, so desperately needed in our diverse urban society, is suffocated under the weight of sometimes ill-conceived and often outdated rules, regulations, controls, and orders. Nobody wins. Organizational values, community concerns, and dedication and devotion to others become lost in a barricaded subculture founded on defensiveness and fear of public and management reprisal—a "we-versus-them" approach.

—Calgary Police Chief Christine Silverberg

A few years ago, Bill Currie chose to back his officers rather than cutting them loose.

"Two of my officers had made public statements amounting to calling Highway 407—the focus of a billion-dollar provincial expenditure to create, then sell, a toll road—unsafe. They spoke from the heart. But there were big headlines. I knew there would be a political price to pay, but I also knew that I would back my officers. They were right, and I said so. Initially, I wasn't believed, the minister of transportation said the OPP don't know what they're talking about. They initiated their own panel of experts, whose recommendations, eleven out of twelve of them, were the OPP's, and the road was closed for four months. There was a further expenditure of $15 million for the safety features we'd asked for. I'm still paying a political price for that, but in the long run it's become a beautiful highway."

In the search for Toronto's new police chief, Mike Boyd and Bill Currie made the short list, along with—according to *The Toronto Star*, and vehemently denied by her—Christine Silverberg. Apparently, at that level, no one really applies, they're "contacted by headhunters," giving everyone a comfortable deniability factor.

Bill Currie withdrew his name, soon after the first *Fifth Estate* profile of Bromell, although he's a little coy about connecting those two events. He'd said to the press that he'd decided to stay with his own folks, but he appreciated having had the opportunity to give the Service his opinions. I cajoled him to tell me, in broad strokes, what he told the interview committee.

"I made six points. I spoke about the appropriate utilization of manpower—where and when and how many officers are deployed. Peak hours are peak hours. You don't have McDonald's, for instance, closing at noon, or busy inventing a new kind of patty while the lineups form, you don't have employees who say, 'I won't work noon hours.' It means breaking down silos and specialties.

"I wanted to look at restructuring the concept of districts. Do field delivery out of four watches, instead of eight divisions. Every officer owns the whole city. You'd have much more flexibility in assigning and moving resources around. Otherwise, administration is multiplied, there is a lot of unnecessary duplication; there are different messages given out in each district, communication suffers. Crooks don't go by districts.

"I spoke about traffic, and how I don't see it primarily as a police issue. It's about roads and engineering and light synchronization and one-way streets; it's about intersections where there is too much of a curve to allow people to go straight through. Fix those things and, if intervention is still necessary, put in cameras.

"Also, the need for a focused message. There's too many people speaking for the Service. The management team is too big; there are too many senior officers. Five deputy chiefs is too many. I would have had me, and one executive deputy chief, the two of us giving out a consistent message. And I spoke about the creation of a value system as the foundation of the Service. A lot of public consultation, an exhaustive consultation, even do a chief's round table with all the players, including the Association, so that everyone would know what our values are. You get people to buy in by example, and by your personal credibility, a demonstrated track record. It wouldn't take long.

"Lastly, I strongly suggested a Toronto-First Policy. Right now, the Toronto Service gets involved everywhere in this province, extending itself beyond its mandate. Training in Kirkland Lake is not necessary; that's what the OPP is there to do. I admit to a bias there," he concludes with a laugh.

I confess that, in contrast to Bill, sometimes when talking to Christine I felt like I was in touch with one of those legendary World War II generals, the corncob-pipe-and-pearl-handled-revolver guys who built up their own mythology alongside their achievements. And why not?

"Every so often in my career, I get this vision, this clarity, where I know exactly what I have to do," Christine said. The woman would look at home running a corporation. She's tailored and ambitious, but she can work a room with warmth.

While she was still working as deputy chief for Hamilton-Wentworth, and resisting the lure of the Calgary headhunters, she was at a meeting of the force's executive, and although, for the life of her, she can't remember the issue that provoked the acrimony, it was a trigger.

"I remember trying to get across, and not succeeding, a different way of looking at the issue. I doubt they ever got it. It's as though I'd leapfrogged eons ahead of where these people were. It all came together for me, and I knew exactly what I had to do. I'm a great believer in destiny."

In her performance appraisals, Christine says her chief would tell her: "The trouble with you, Christine, is that you can see the issues and be so far ahead, come to the right conclusions, but people aren't ready, they're still at square one."

"I have pretty clear visions of the future, and know all the pieces that have to be put together to achieve it, but it's very hard to get people to think in these terms. Sometimes I want to say: 'You don't get it, you don't see!'

"You might think that being chief means being able to fix those things you've noticed on your way up."

Apparently not, at least not right away.

"You can't just shout out your door, 'Change has occurred.' Unless it's properly introduced and handled, it can lead to disaster. You have to build the capacity of the organization to change, and it takes a lot of cultivation."

Her most frustrating moments come about through the bureaucratic mindset.

"When I was first starting this job, I had a letter from a constable who had a child playing—quite well—in a local hockey league. He went to all his kid's games. And sometimes he coached as well. Things would sometimes get a bit rocky, with the parents egging on their kids. He was essentially asking for permission to wear his uniform to the games, give a little law-and-order presence. I sent it to my executive, the deputy chief, and the answer came back, no. I asked why not, and I was told it would be against policy. What policy? They told me, and I asked if anyone knew why the policy was created and who created it. The chief, they said. Wait a minute, I said. I'm the chief.

"It took eight months, but I kept grinding away. They'd say there were worker's compensation issues, paid duty claims, liability issues, union issues. One by one I knocked off the objections. It was amazing, how the automatic response was, 'No, it would break the rules.'"

It sounds like a chapter out of *Yes, Minister*, the British comedy dealing with the techniques of bureaucrats to maintain the status quo, no matter what politician is in office. From the relatively unimportant changes to the serious ones, obstructions will be put up. The danger is we might become satisfied with that snail's pace of reform, take pleasure in small victories.

Christine went out and talked with frontline cops, to get a sense of the people she was leading and for them to get to know her.

"I tried to take it to the simplest level: What kind of organization do you want to work for and live in? I made it very clear in talking to the front line—who spent most of the time talking about the problems—that I could create a systems structure, a framework, for them to solve those problems, but that when I come back to them in two years, I want to see that you have."

Not every new chief works out. Ken Higgins retired just as the new chief (hired away from Thunder Bay, Ontario, where he was well-liked) who's since left the job, was coming on, but Ken was watching and listening.

He'll only speak in generalities, not comment specifically on this former chief. "Some people will say, 'Why go outside the force?' It's standard. Vancouver itself has supplied leaders for other departments, it's just part of that level of policing. We can't say no outsiders here and at the same time demand the right to apply elsewhere.

"For a new guy, there's often a rush around, getting to know the organization, and part of that involves riding along with members of the force, putting real pictures to the problems you read about. It's a balancing act, interminable meetings, helping the force and the public get to know who the chief is, and the real job—which is providing the best level of service—ensuring your men and women have the best equipment and working conditions.

"Ultimately, it's about the acquisition of resources. You're up against all other city departments and their demands for increased service.

"Although political correctness would have the community put first, it's the department that should come first—ensuring that you have a well-staffed, well-run cohesive force. As well, you have to have effective community relations; effective enforcement; proactive, community-based programs; effective follow-up; and targeted enforcement in trafficking and breaking-and-entering."

Christine Silverberg sees the same kind of tensions in the job. "Our citizens for example, have told us they want to be more involved in policing decisions that affect them. They are concerned about certain kinds of crime and disorder, such as domestic violence, child abuse, youth violence, and traffic safety—and they want increased emphasis on prevention, intervention, and apprehension. Our employees told me they want a flexible reporting structure, improved communications, tolerance of experimentation, programs for self-development, opportunities for career development, an ability to identify and resolve their own issues, and to participate in decision-making around those issues, and a caring leadership.

"Our police commission wants a strong commitment to community policing, cost-effectiveness and efficiency in the operation of the police service, increased workforce capability, and accountability.

"And our external environment is one of economic restraint and fiscal accountability, growth in an increasingly diverse society, ongoing legislative changes that create enormous stresses to change and adapt quickly, and access to information, communications technology, and technological changes that create still further demand for new systems and structures."

As far as discipline goes, Christine Silverberg claims, "If you want your officers to take risks, there must be some toleration of mistakes—but not those mistakes that offend core values or show a lack of integrity or honesty."

Members of police forces must understand, and their leaders must demonstrate, that those core values are not simply written for public consumption, a kind of comfortable window-dressing, but are meant to be followed throughout their careers. They are not optional, depending on circumstances or neighbourhoods.

I believe we have failed to make that clear.

PRIORITIES
"Yep, it was stolen"

Ken Higgins was involved in strategic planning for the Vancouver force, and he notes that "If you or I were running a bank, setting grand strategy, we'd be dropping this or that, selling off some things, changing direction. That's the one thing never heard in policing—dropping things. We've kept everything we've ever been charged with, and kept adding other things, and the resources simply don't match the growth.

"If you're a hard-nosed executive with a Board that will back you, you've got to get out of certain things and redeploy in others. For instance, not having a dedicated traffic division. Getting rid of the expensive "hayburners," those horses and riders the public like so much, and put the cops on bicycles. If you have seventeen officers in schools, doing liaison, the schools should be paying for them, or put them back on the road."

He adds that there are some exceptions.

"The police no longer send a squad car to check out a stolen-car report an hour later, to essentially say, 'Yep, there's no car in the driveway'—'Yep, it was stolen.'"

With all its unaddressed big-city problems, and fights over sufficient resources, the big current issue of the day in Toronto—probably out of all proportion—is raves, dance parties where no alcohol is permitted, but drugs like ecstasy find a huge market. Toronto's police have set up a special taskforce to deal with the high-profile raves, no doubt pulling away resources from the streets.

The Ontario government decided to tackle the "pressing" issue of squeegee kids, passing a law to enable the police to ticket street kids who offer to clean windshields of motorists at intersections—sometimes quite insistently. It was a popular move in many sectors but prompted the question, How do street kids, many of whom are runaways from abusive homes, earn enough money to stay alive?

Issuing fines to children who don't make enough money to eat, never mind house themselves, is a clear attempt to reduce their visibility, to encourage them to move on to more tolerant cities, out of sight, out of mind, making the streets more comfortable for the rest of us, the more fortunate.

Bill Currie would have put them in uniforms, paid them out of the city budget, demanded a level of civility, and provided a free service to motorists, which could have been quite popular, especially in winter.

POLICIES AND PRACTICES

"A lot of people out there with circuit damage"

In this country, the reaction to crime statistics rivals the controversy over where to draw the poverty line. It seems that in order to get the resources a chief feels he or she needs, high crime is a definite boost. Rampant crime clearly dictates increased resources to deal with it.

Incoming Toronto Chief Fantino was criticized in the "liberal press" for timely remarks about lawlessness. By all accounts, the crime rate is down overall.

But to Ken Higgins "The public uses crime stats the way a drunk uses a street lamp, for support, not light."

Ken believes, and Fantino would probably agree, that in spite of the lower crime levels reported, the escalating level of violence, the degree of viciousness, in the commission of a crime doesn't show in the statistics.

"There's a lot of people out there who seem to have circuit damage—much more attuned to and prepared to be violent," says Ken.

He doesn't think that the falling murder rate reflects much either, except that our paramedics and emergency wards have gotten a lot better at saving lives, stabilizing victims at the scene, so that critical injuries, which would have resulted in death even five years ago, now are survivable.

"Who could have envisioned that our movies would turn into large cartoon-style portrayals of constant violence, with graphic murders every few moments? Our good old brains never forget anything they see, and if someone has a lot of trouble sorting out reality from fiction, it can implant scenarios that—left to their own devices—they never would have thought of. Even television situation comedies seem to reward rude and boorish behaviours towards siblings and parents. It's seen as witty and clever. Civility is not highly prized any more."

Ken also believes a lot of crime goes unreported, including himself in that category: "My own police car was parked outside a hotel during the OPEC conference, and in spite of the lights and markings they smashed the window and stole my raincoat."

It is true that as a result of our failure to deal with poverty, addictions, and the growing numbers of the homeless, whole communities of the dispossessed are becoming brutalized by hand-to-mouth existences, and—in order to stay alive—these people have to operate by the rules of the street, which are harsh and unforgiving. Violence is always an immediate threat, especially to these increasingly vulnerable populations who are preyed upon by the slightly stronger, the more ruthless, those who live by exploiting or stealing from those whose weakness makes them easy targets.

Fledgling serial killers know instinctively that victimizing prostitutes will ensure their crimes will go almost unnoticed for some time, till they're ready to graduate to the mainstream population.

Having worked with street people, with hookers with no skills or education to improve their lot in life, with young men who exist on the number of B&Es they can commit, with dealers who sell to feed their own habits, it is clear to me that arrest and jail time is viewed as a kind of government tax on their existence. Jail at least provides a bed and three meals a day, as well as enhancing the individual's street reputation.

What offends us is not the fact of poverty or homelessness as much as the signs of it. We make laws about urinating or defecating in public spaces, or littering with used condoms or needles in parks, and send our police to enforce those laws.

Mike Boyd and Bob Kerr feel that if we just treated everyone with the same degree of professionalism, no matter what their skin colour or sexual orientation or economic status, we'd go a long way to achieving a higher level of trust.

Fantino has announced his intention to change the colour and style of Toronto's police uniforms, at the same time ridding the force of the more casual baseball caps—to help the force look more professional and to protect them from standing out, in the street lights, in dangerous situations. The force will move to black pants and black shirts.

Bill Currie, some years ago, tried to argue the need to move away from the paramilitary look, especially in the American-style caps worn by the OPP. He lost that vote.

Peggy Gamble likes the look. She feels that if three officers are standing together they should be indistinguishable from one another, the same crease in their pants, the same tilt of the hat.

Looking around your own city, at how security guards are outfitted, you may have noticed how closely they ape the garb of real cops. I've seen security dressed like British Special Forces, in black outfits. Now it appears Toronto cops will be trying to look like security guards.

The danger is that clothes, as they say, make the man. A paramilitary look edges us back to Command and Control, a mindset not conducive to community policing. Police won't act more professionally just because they're dressed in black, with no soft edges. (Not to mention it's really hard to get powdered sugar off the shirts and trousers.)

We have seen how long it takes to get police to behave in a professional manner with one another, to accept diversity in their ranks—never mind in the communities they patrol—to hold one another accountable for "actions unbecoming." This is mostly due to the leadership of the services and their reluctance to ensure that mission and value statements are seen as more than lip service to an unreasonable public.

Chiefs are highly politicized these days, walking a tightrope between the various expectations Christine has outlined and trying to keep internal peace. The last thing a chief needs is to be seen as someone who cannot control his officers. Politicians won't hold Police Services to account—it's too risky. The anti-cop label can be a career killer, especially in our era of intolerance for "crime" and "visibility."

Chiefs need to be very clear, and very believable, with their officers on what constitutes professionalism in the 21st century. They cannot have one showcase policy for public consumption and an internal one that suggests business as usual, such as we have now. Police officers are public servants and must be held to at least the same standards as any other public body. Unions have built their strength on resistance to new expectations and new definitions of what makes a good cop. A kind of internal Reform party, clinging to the bad old days and bad old ways. No force can tolerate two chiefs, one appointed by the Services Board and one elected by the union.

There are so many good cops who've been failed by those who lead them, who've been silenced by their brethren. The Blue Wall of Silence is a piece of mythology that belongs in the past; it protects only those not worth protecting; it drags down the standards of the force, it is the refuge of scoundrels.

Education in diversity, in "the soft skills," as well as crisis-intervention training, has to be made mandatory, with no exceptions, up and down the ranks. Chiefs need to set the example by attending themselves, along with their senior executives. They need to speak to the rank and file, off the public record, so that the officers understand that times have indeed changed, along with expectations.

Police need much more exposure to people outside the force, which most do not get in their regular lives—most cops socialize only with other cops. Bringing in plenty of civilians as volunteers, as educators, as workers, might help to achieve that, might break into the institutionalized perceptions of just who is out there. What would also help is to have police education and training in public colleges and universities, rather than closed systems in a police academy.

We have to stop pussyfooting around their egos and likes and dislikes and establish a zero tolerance where it can do the most good. And make sure it happens.

Some of our lives depend on it.

Profiles

I didn't expect to care so much about the men and women who shared their experiences with me. My usual beat is poverty, mental illness, and addictions; I thought this—in comparison—would be a bit of an emotional cakewalk, interesting but not about to affect me on a personal level. I was wrong. It's impossible not to care.

The women who broke down the doors to join the force are unheralded in the feminist movement, but what a journey they went on—what they endured, with very little notice from superiors—to be able to don the uniform!

Men like Currie and Higgins, with their sense of honour and duty, their intellect and empathy, would shine in any position they chose in society. They chose the police force.

The simple yet extraordinary courage shown by Jay Hope and Karen Bell, the belief in the duty to serve and protect epitomized by Peggy Gamble. These are not the stereotypes that spring to mind when we hear the word "cops."

They deserve our assistance to bring the forces up to

the standards they set—not drag them down to the level of the worst cops we encounter.

When someone is wearing a uniform, especially a police uniform, it's hard to see that person as someone with a mother and father; it's difficult to imagine a cop as an ordinary kid, doing regular stuff; it's almost impossible to find individuality. But police aren't born clutching miniature clubs or powdered doughnuts.

During my initial interviews, I invited each cop to tell me about his or her early life, about their families and communities, and about their decision to make policing a career.

KEN HIGGINS, VANCOUVER POLICE DEPUTY CHIEF (RETIRED)

Ken Higgins grew up in Thomas Hardy country in England, launching miniature gliders from the hills near his village home, then chasing after them on his bike. Over the year or so I was working on this book, we talked a great deal. He was generous and thoughtful with his answers. He seemed to come from a different time, a simpler time, when words like honour and duty didn't sound stilted and strange. In many ways, the world he grew up in doesn't exist anymore, and there's a great sadness in that.

Life as a child for him meant school five days a week, delivering the evening paper, going to choir practice on Friday evenings, and to church twice on Sundays. His family lived in a large, brick three-bedroom house, which everyone called a cottage; his father worked the garden year round and during the week worked as a machinist in one of the town's light industries. They didn't have a car, but they did have two upright pianos, one for practice and one for good.

"We were quite musical, and the three of us kids used to clean up at local concerts. I'd win singing prizes for my boy-soprano voice; my brother would win for piano playing; and my sister a bit of both."

On Saturdays, he'd meet his girlfriend, now his wife, in town (she lived in a nearby village) and they'd spend his paper-route money on espresso coffee or a picture show.

At sixteen, he was already a qualified glider pilot, thanks to two years in air cadets; he got that before his driver's licence, for which you had to be seventeen. It was, for him, a toss-up—the air force or the police.

At that time, the police had realized that waiting till the age of nineteen to recruit meant missing a number of likely candidates who would already have embarked on their life choices. The police had instituted a cadet program, which meant a "combination of exposure to academic subjects, attending college as day attendees, but not full time, a lot of physical fitness and training, such as Outward Bound programs, and a life lived in a small, monk-like cell of a room, pretty self-contained except for communal shower facilities."

There had been concerns about his leaving his small rural village—where many of the residents had never been further than fifty miles from their homes—and travelling

150 miles to London. The last Sunday before he left, the minister said a prayer for his well-being and privately hinted at some of the temptations he might be exposed to and must avoid, which of course piqued his interest.

It was with some disappointment then, to a sixteen-year-old, as his first experience of the big city, to have his hair cut off and then be sent "to spend a few weeks with other new cadets slogging around Dartmoor with a heavy pack."

BILL CURRIE, ONTARIO PROVINCIAL POLICE DEPUTY COMMISSIONER

Bill Currie is my personal yardstick for what makes a good cop and a good leader. In some ways, he and Ken Higgins have a lot in common—in their broad range of interests, in the women they married, in their ambition and political astuteness. Both men are eminently civilized in their approaches to policing, in their awareness of the privilege and responsibility that goes with the job.

Bill's father went into the army almost immediately following Bill's birth in 1941, starting as a signalman, and rising to training staff sergeant. He was posted to Victoria, then Jamaica for training, then was slated for Hong Kong. But he was called off the boat, his talents needed here, and he never got overseas. Back home, he worked for Mutual and Federated Life Insurance.

"My mother was a real people person, my father much more restrained. You knew he loved you, but he wasn't demonstrative about it. My mother raised me those first few years."

She'd also worked during the war to keep the family in food and clothing.

Bill found a mentor in his father's brother, Norm, who became president and CEO of Maple Leaf Foods.

"My father was quite proud of his younger brother's success. And Norm became an excellent role model for me, especially in his dislike of management concentrated in little boxes. He banned job descriptions. I never met anyone who didn't like him."

In 1949, Bill's father was determined to get the kids out of the city and away from the polio epidemic that had gripped the community. They ended up in a cottage on Six Mile Lake, in Muskoka, and that as much as anything shaped his personality and outlook.

He had a paper route early in life, one hundred *Globe and Mail*s to deliver in the mornings; and at thirteen he ran a huge water-taxi. Bill's dad had had to quit high school as a teenager to help support his family, and this matter-of-fact personal sacrifice showed in his relationship with his son. Bill still remembers one summer in his teens when he worked at a marina, and there the policy was to hold back their entire pay till Labour Day. He came home, and his dad said, "We're a little short right now, we can use it."

"I had to hand it over. It was a little traumatic, but I got over it in a couple of hours."

Bill played hockey at St. Michael's, a goalie in the days before face masks, and he didn't expect and never got driven to the games; he'd lug all his equipment on the streetcar. He still wonders, being the hockey fanatic he still is, how far he might have gone with a little more encouragement. But he knows he lacked the single-minded focus of a Gretzky, and at the time each of the six NHL teams only had one full-time goalie, not the fifty or so positions in today's NHL.

He remembers his dad buying him his first car when he was sixteen; it was pretty much a wreck, but Bill was told if you can fix it, you can have it. The car turned a nearby white picket fence black when he turned on the engine. He'd run his friends to hockey games at St. Mike's, each chum putting in a nickel. Thirty-five cents bought enough gas for two days.

The Curries had the first television in their neighbourhood, a ten-inch black-and-white set surrounded "by yards of cabinet"; reflecting a tendency to hang on to things. His parents gave it to him and his wife Doreen after they married in '62.

Bill taught at inner-city schools and moved up to vice-principal but after fifteen years was feeling restless and somewhat besieged.

"I was tired of trying to change things, so I decided to go somewhere I had no chance at all of changing policy," he grins. To hear him tell it, it was the idea of escaping from the people and their constant demands at his school. Driving alone in a cool car along Ontario's highways was what initially attracted him, he told me. I suspect he was plain fed up.

He'd served as a chief negotiator for the Catholic teachers in 1970 when he was vice-principal.

"We were vastly underpaid, but it wasn't a greed thing. I promised them a 35 percent increase over one year. I led their first one-day walkout ever. I was able to get 41 percent over two years, which was pretty good, but when I announced it to the union meeting at the Exhibition Coliseum, they pelted me with stuff, like 'What the hell good is that?' I learned to be careful then about highballing expectations though it had helped me to get the 41 percent."

He knew that starting a new career at this stage of his life was taking a big risk, but he didn't want to stagnate behind school walls. He was thirty-four, one moment an educator, the next a 4th-class constable (earning $15,000 less a year) living in a dormitory with thirty others, all of whom were an average of ten years younger.

JOHN IRWIN, TORONTO POLICE SERGEANT

John was twelve years old when his father was shot and killed. Losing a father in any circumstances is difficult enough, but it's especially difficult when your dad is a cop and is killed on duty. Like most cops, John minimizes the pain he went through, using humour often; but in many ways he doesn't think like a "typical cop."

"A call went out for a uniform constable to check out someone firing a pellet gun at cars along the Don Valley

Parkway. My dad and his partner—both detectives—didn't feel he should respond to that call alone, so they both went. They were big men. When they got into the apartment building and walked down the hallway, there was nowhere to hide, and no way to miss them. The guy, whose record was just fraud, nothing violent, had been drinking. He had a .22, not a pellet gun, and he's muttering, he's going to 'beat the Johns [slang at the time for cops] at their own game,' and I think my father was a pacifist; he tried to talk to the guy, get him to put the weapon down, but in seconds the guy shot my dad and his partner. Both collapsed, fatally wounded, in the corridor. The constable had been able to duck in a doorway, till the guy ran, then he chased him down the stairs where the guy took off outside. Then the constable ran back up and was attempting CPR on my dad, who was still breathing, when the shooter came back, weapon in hand, and the cop shot him dead."

He remembers being woken in the middle of the night by his uncle, who told his brother and him that their dad had been in an accident and their mom was on the way to the hospital; they were to go with him to his house.

"My dad had been in an accident that same year, got a concussion and was in hospital for a while, then signed himself out and came home. So we kind of thought, my brother and I, as we piled into the back of my uncle's squad car, that it was the same kind of deal. We were young, and it was really exciting to be driving in a cop car, a major big deal.

"At my uncle's, my aunt was listening to the radio, and

a bulletin came on that two officers had been shot. And I remember thinking, gee, that's sad. On the news they were saying they couldn't release the names yet because of notification of next of kin, but later on, right on the radio, they gave out my dad's name and his partner's. Even then, being shot, well, as a kid you thought of John Wayne with a bullet in him getting back on his horse, we had no idea how serious this was. We played with our cousins most of the day, till my mom got back from the hospital, and we got called into the living room, everyone standing around, telling us our dad was dead."

John's parents had had a deep love between them. He remembers how they used to push back the furniture, roll up the carpet in the living room, and dance. It was the late sixties, they'd already been married nearly twenty years, but they were that close.

"None of my friends' parents were like that."

He learned about strength, standing up for yourself, and morality from both his parents. That you didn't just go along to fit in. If something's wrong, you say so. But not the kind of morality that exists simply to judge others.

"If my father had not been killed, I probably—like most kids—wouldn't have cared less what he thought. After his death, it was natural to idealize him, to ask myself what my father would have thought or done in certain situations. Two things I knew for sure: If I have a loaf of bread and someone's hungry, share it. And don't judge others until you walk in their shoes."

They lived in Don Mills, and though they hung out

with the rough kids, roughness was purely relative: "We're not talking Regent Park rough, though some got done for drugs later on."

He remembers how he handled being offered drugs: "I had to stand up, like I was taught, and say, no, not for me. I'm leaving, and anyone else who wants to leave with me is welcome."

He'd grown up listening to his dad talk about his day, "Not the gory, gruesome stuff, but we had a pretty good idea of the job and the people he'd encounter during his shift." These conversations were usually over breakfast if his dad had worked the midnight shift. He'd stay up to eat with his kids, not going to bed till they'd left for school.

For a while John vacillated between being a dentist ("our dentist was a really nice guy") or a lawyer or a cop, but six years after the shooting, at the age of eighteen, he passed the physical and written tests and joined the police cadets. His mother took it well, only asking him whether he was doing it to follow his father or because it was something he really wanted to do. He doesn't regret his decision.

PEGGY GAMBLE, ONTARIO PROVINCIAL POLICE SERGEANT

Peggy always wanted to be a cop. "Since I was seven years old, playing at home with my five brothers and one sister, I'd always be the cop, and they'd be the bad guys." Her mother's father had been a cop, in England, and though she never met him, she remembers great stories.

By the time she was eighteen, she wanted to get away from home, but Toronto held no allure for her. She liked the friendlier atmosphere of a smaller town, where everybody knows everybody. She chose Sudbury's Cambrian College, and found herself doing a placement at the Sudbury jail a minimum security place that occasionally held medium and maximum security prisoners.

"I hated it. For twelve hours a day, it felt like you were locked up with them."

She moved to Cambridge, Ontario and attended the University of Waterloo and worked for a year in a lumber mill making lattice and cutting lumber for shipping. She also worked for a time as a bartender in her brother's bar.

Peggy chose the OPP because of their recruiting brochure. It looked more diverse—from the pictures—and she thought there would be more ability to do different things, more chances for promotion, and the ability to specialize.

Imagine applying for a job and having to bring your family in for an interview. Imagine having to supply a list of your friends. Her father, a machinist, was still living when this happened, and was pleased that she had realized her ambition. Her mother had died of cancer when Peggy was twenty-two, two months before she signed up. Her father has since died, of a heart attack, in October 1996.

In her patrol car, ranging the highways of the GTA, Peggy seems to have found her calling.

JEFF MCARTHUR, RCMP CONSTABLE

Jeff moved around a lot as a child. His dad was a bank manager and was transferred every few years. With his parents and two sisters, he lived in Victoria, Whitehorse, Chiliwack, Toronto, and Calgary.

"I'm sure a lot of the people you're talking to were real bright lights, all-star this and that, in sports or academically. But I was an average performer, a bit of an awkward kid. Somewhere between the outcasts and the in-crowd."

In Calgary, he applied to the RCMP, but it turned out to be bad timing. "They had a hiring freeze; only women, French Canadians, and ethnic minorities were making it in."

There was a back-door approach Jeff heard about—and took—that of Special Constable. He received nine weeks' training after he was accepted. "Mostly, in my class, it was older people, in their forties or fifties, who already had a career, or white Anglo-Saxon Protestant kids like me—cop wannabes—who couldn't get into the force directly."

Later transferred to Vancouver, he found guarding consulates and embassies a profoundly boring job. He spent his nights upgrading his education, taking a joint philosophy-psychology major at UBC, hoping the time would come when he could be a real cop. Ultimately, his perseverance paid off.

Jeff's the kind of cop who loves going after bad guys; loves the hunt, the chase, the catch, the nights filled with adrenaline and danger.

MIKE BOYD,
TORONTO POLICE DEPUTY CHIEF

Mike Boyd struck me as a very careful man. Over the course of our interviews, if a question seemed a bit leading or tricky, I could practically hear him thinking hard during the pauses. I had expected this from the men and women I talked to but, for the most part, didn't encounter it. I assume it's his position that makes him cautious. On the other hand, he's a man who loves to learn and, I think, loves to teach.

Mike was born to working-class parents and has lived all his life within the boundaries of Metro Toronto. His father worked as a blacksmith—officially called a blacksmith/welder by his employer (the city of Toronto)—and his mom worked for the postal service.

Mike went to school in Scarborough and was very active in hockey and sports generally. Like Ken Higgins, his was a musical family: His grandfather played violin, his father the guitar. Mike joined the school band and, dropping sports, gravitated more towards music. By the time the Beatles burst onto the scene, he had his own band, playing that kind of music. "I even had the haircut."

His family didn't have much in terms of material things, but his was a sound home, where he was given "a good, moral upbringing. I was a conformist in school, never in trouble, always doing what I was told. I wanted to meet the expectations of my parents and teachers."

He'd never actually thought about becoming a cop, but

he met a retired officer, who'd moved into the business community, who told him it was a good job to get into.

"I also had some expectations of what a police officer should be—it's a great opportunity to help people and do good things. My parents were surprised when I told them what I wanted to be, since I'd never spoken about police work, but they were very proud: policing was an honourable career."

TOBY HINTON,
VANCOUVER POLICE CONSTABLE

Toby Hinton was more of a hellraiser. He believes the police force made him a better person. He was attracted to it after reading Joseph Wambaugh's books, and he knew immediately that that was the life for him.

His parents had moved from Vancouver to a "redneck logging town called Chemainus, on the east coast of Vancouver Island, with the third-largest lumber mill in the world, and a population of 3,000. They'd thought it was a way to protect their children from unhealthy influences, but Chemainus was also the beer-drinking capital of Canada."

If you weren't involved in sports, there wasn't much to do except raise hell, and for a teenager, "Idle time equals devil's play. You should see the place today, it's been revitalized through murals. You can go there for a nostalgic tour, and these big portraits of cheery, smiling loggers are everywhere. There's nothing glorious, in my memory, about fishing and logging, it's hard work."

He outgrew the small town at seventeen, moving to Northern Ontario, working on the railroad. He was in a holding pattern and very unhappy. He'd applied to the RCMP and "Things were going fine till they checked with the local constabulary in my home town. I could picture them laughing themselves silly as they pitched my application into the wastebasket. I was devastated. I couldn't translate my university degree into work I enjoyed, so I pulled the pin and came back to Vancouver with my girlfriend. We got work, establishing and running a group home for children in Mackenzie, an end-of-the-road mill town in the British Columbia interior. I remember we carried a $12,000 cheque to furnish this big, empty house."

Children with varying degrees of trouble, from fetal alcohol syndrome to ten-year-old gasoline sniffers, would have short-term stays; Toby and his lady lived in the basement. It wasn't a job he would ever have considered on his own, and his frustrations grew. After a year in the house, he sent out applications to every police force he could think of.

"I remember flying in for an interview in Victoria, but after thirty seconds I knew it was over. I'd gotten started on the wrong foot, and all I could do was hunker down and try to get out with some dignity. But then Vancouver came through, and I went for a fairly long interview with the recruiting sergeant. I connected with him. One of his early questions was: Had I had any run-ins with the law? I went through absolutely everything I could remember. You don't understand as a kid how badly your actions can affect your future. For instance, when we were in our late teens, a friend and I were going to surprise a fellow who'd flown in from the interior and was coming in by ferry to attend his girlfriend's graduation. We wanted to get to him first, so that we'd have a couple of hours of drinking before we'd drop him off at the grad dance. We'd stopped for gas, and that station was running a promo for pantyhose, and the attendant had thrown in a pair. So we decided to put on stocking masks, and we grabbed him off the ferry dock. We struggled, fake struggling, because by then he knew who we were, and we bundled him into the van and took off, aiming to stop at a liquor store. That done, we got back in the van and ran smack into a huge roadblock, and a major take-down. We didn't know what the hell was happening: We kept asking, what's this all about?

"The cops eventually just called us jackasses and let us go, but the information was now on file, a permanent record. The RCMP have this system called PIRS (Personal Information Retrieval System), and if you've come into any contact with them, even if it's casual, it can be entered.

"After I'd finish disclosing all this negative stuff, the recruiting sergeant said 'Good, I'm glad you told me,' showing me a printout from the RCMP that detailed all I'd confessed to. He also said: 'I don't consider this reflective of anything but a bit of youthful stupidity,' and asked me to help him sell me as a recruit: volunteer work, references, anything that would make me look good. I had to have about thirty references, my friends and neighbours were interviewed."

He was given his chance. And then there was the lie-detector test.

"It was fairly new then, just introduced, and they covered a wide range of topics. Mostly they were looking for inconsistencies from your first interview, if all your answers had been truthful. I went in thinking it was no big deal, I was mentally stronger than any machine, but they showed you right off how good that machine was. They handed you a deck of cards, told you to chose one and put it back in the pack. You were then supposed to lie about what that card was, and that damn machine knew right away. My 'at rest' heart-beat is 60. The examiner told me I was at an average of 120 for the duration of the test.

"I'm an adult. I've lived a life. If I were recruiting, I wouldn't look for someone who hasn't really lived, and therefore has a limited world view. Once you're out there, where there's a whole sea of grays, very little black and white, how would an inexperienced person cope?"

Toby, who could be used as a poster boy for recruiting drives, and his partner, Al Arsenault, make up the core of the Odd Squad, an innovative effort on the streets of Vancouver.

AL ARSENAULT,
VANCOUVER POLICE CONSTABLE

Al, Toby Hinton's partner, comes from a family of seven, with a very loving mother, and a father who seemed to have no time for his children. A troubled teenager, at thirteen he made a court appearance that scared him enough to straighten him out. He knows now that his acting out was aimed squarely at his dad, who was a probation officer: "It's just like the old saying: The painter's house has the worst paint job."

There was physical abuse, one of the reasons for his life-long interest in the martial arts—not for exacting revenge, but to ensure he'd be able to defend himself. His dad had had an abusive relationship with his own father; things get passed on. By the time Al was in his twenties, their relationship had improved a great deal and is still very strong. He's grateful to his parents for instilling in him strong values and a good work ethic. With a B.Sc. and a B.Ed., (double honours in geology and geography), Al is an educated man.

"I loved rocks, and collected them as a kid. But I knew I was too much of a socialite to spend my life in the bush."

He'd thought about teaching as a career, but at the time there weren't many openings—and he looked at his brother who was stuck substitute teaching, a different school every few days. He didn't know a lot about policing, or what they actually did; there weren't a ton of cop shows like there are now. What he did know was that he needed to move outside the cloistered academic environment, and policing seemed a good way of "advancing both my shooting skills and my social skills." He also wanted the kind of job that would not box him in, in terms of social mobility, one that would satisfy a kind of societal voyeurism.

He was snapped up by the Vancouver police when he applied.

Al is about as honest as a guy can get and about as politically incorrect. He's brash, cocky, and a real street cop.

CHRISTINE SILVERBERG, CALGARY POLICE CHIEF

Christine was raised on a farm north of Brampton, Ontario, with her two older brothers and a much younger sister. She went to a one-room schoolhouse and wasn't allowed to date until she was sixteen. But she did have a boyfriend.

"I don't know if this is relevant: I didn't even realize it at the time, but he was black. He played sax in my brother's band. My mother had never been one to make distinctions between people, certainly not based on race."

Christine didn't start out wanting to be a cop. She met her future husband while she was an undergraduate at Glendon College (York University) almost thirty years ago. Aside from the time she drank some blackberry brandy, she managed to avoid the temptations that arose from being away from home. "Certainly some students were into drugs, but many kids weren't. Sometimes I think I pass my life not paying attention to those kinds of things."

It was natural for her to go out to work while her husband finished his degree. She'd heard of an opening at the Vanier Centre for women, where people sentenced to two years less a day served their time. The Ontario government of the day had a philosophy emphasizing the modification of behaviour and attitudes: Residents were housed in cottages, around a central hub. Although there was male security on the grounds, corrections officers were not to carry weapons; so the only thing she had to get herself out of trouble was her ability to diffuse tension. Two officers per shift worked one cottage, housing about twenty-five residents. Many of the women had severe drug and alcohol problems and had spent long stretches in Kingston Pen.

It was clear to her that a lot of the trouble the inmates had gotten into occurred because of the men with whom they were involved. It also became apparent how insane it was to attempt to modify the attitudes of inmates using a middle-class framework that would have no relevance when they returned to lives that were anything but. She got quite passionate over this: cooking and sewing instead of learning anger management, group therapy where women had twenty-four hours to come up with things to say. She understood that more important than anything else was the exercise of common sense.

"I'm not sure that at the time I had a real sense of what a criminal was. It was also the first time I'd encountered lesbianism, as well as a lot of words I'd never heard before. I was nineteen, twenty years old."

Christine felt that one of the things that served her well was an inherent understanding of the need to help women on a very fundamental level. With rare exceptions she remembers, the other officers were quite cynical.

"They didn't have a real sense of caring—not caring in a fluffy sense. You need to respond to the whole person, not be just didactic or scripted in your dealings with them."

After Vanier, she applied to the Mississauga police force and was accepted.

KAREN BELL, ANISHINABEK POLICE SERVICES SERGEANT

Karen is, in many ways a survivor, against incredible odds. Like Christine Silverberg, Karen also grew up on an isolated farm (though that's where the similarities end) at Bell's Point, on the Garden River Reserve outside of Sault Ste. Marie, Ontario. Here was once a trading post, before the signing of the treaties, and it "was given to my family long ago as a way of protecting the reserve—the Bells watching one end, the Pines the other."

Her father was raised at Bell's Point—now a trailer park—and her mother was brought up on the reserve; when Karen was growing up, her nearest neighbour was a mile away. There was no running water, no electricity. Four boys and four girls were born to her mother, often only a year apart. The kids were very close. They had only each other to play with. They were not really accepted on the reserve, being seen as too remote to be a regular part of life there. Karen couldn't go to kindergarten on the reserve, as there was no bus; most kids lived within walking distance, but for her it would have meant trudging seven miles.

By the time she was ready for grade one, she still had to walk a quarter of a mile, in winter over snowdrifts, to get to the highway, where the bus would pick her up. She was the first one on and the last one off. The bus had about forty kids by the time they reached the school in Sault Ste. Marie, and at first she remembers being excited and happy.

"We all went to the same Catholic school, and most of the students were native. I mostly remember that the teachers were really mean. Back then, parents had no involvement in the schools, there was no PTA; discipline and education were left to the teachers. Your parents expected you to learn and behave. I remember getting the leather strap in grade one but don't recall for what. I was so scared. I wouldn't get out of the desk; I just froze to it, and they had to drag the desk halfway down the corridor before I let go. Another time, I'd forgotten to bring my lunch, and they sent me home. I remember walking the miles to Garden River, along Highway 17. I got there about the same time as the school bus was bringing the other kids home."

Her father worked shifts at the steel mill in town, as well as working the farm with his wife; they kept cows and horses and raised corn. "I had a fairly good upbringing. I wasn't exposed to alcohol or wife-beating early in my life."

But when Karen was eleven, her mother started going

out to bingo and not coming home till really late at night, drunk. Her father responded initially by locking his wife out, and finally, when the behaviour persisted, kicking her out. She was gone, taking only her oldest daughter, for the next five years. She was thirty-two years old, with a kid born every year, with a husband seven, eight years older—she was isolated, bored, wrung out.

"No letters, no postcards, nothing for five years," Karen remembers. The youngest child at home was less than a year old. It seemed natural and necessary to take over the role her mother had abandoned.

"I have a vague memory of someone from Children's Aid visiting us, but there were no supports then, and they left my dad and us on our own. There was no choice for me, if we were to stay together. I cooked two meals a day, did the laundry, with pump water heated up, made sure the chores got done. By that time, I was in grade seven or eight. I had become kind of like his partner."

And a victim of incest as well. She was twelve when it began.

"I can remember lying in bed—there were only two bedrooms, one for the girls, one for the boys—being really scared. I knew it wasn't right. I can remember trying to be sexually pleasing to him so he wouldn't touch the others."

She told a native counsellor what was happening, and all the children were sent to a receiving home in the city. That wasn't what she wanted. Who would adopt seven kids? She didn't want her father sent to jail; she just wanted him to stop. And he did, though the damage was done.

Like most sexually abused kids, sex became the only way of being loved, and by the time she was fifteen she was pregnant by a twenty-five-year-old Garden River man. She kept the secret for five months—it was her father who noticed and took her to a doctor, saying something like: Look what you've done to yourself.

She was shipped off by bus to a home for unwed mothers in Toronto, and she remembers being met at the station by one of the nuns who ran the place. She hated it; no one called, no one came to see her. Her father had told her: Don't come home with a baby. The baby was born with a heart defect, she signed his baptismal certificate and a permission form for his operation at the same time. The Children's Aid Society convinced her it would be better to give him up; he probably wouldn't live to see his fifth birthday.

She couldn't stay at the home anymore; other unwed mothers needed her bed; so she returned to Garden River, where, for a while, it seemed everyone was pointing to her, calling her a slut and worse.

Life started getting better for her in grade ten. She started making friends through sports and clubs, some of them from the large Italian population of the Sault. She was an average student who had enormous difficulty with math; she had to do grade ten math four times, but she loved to read and still does. Back then, it was an escape and a way of learning how other people lived.

Karen speaks almost clinically about her early life, and she knows it. That remove still affects relationships. "I've never had another child, never married. I can be distant; I have real problems opening up, trusting, I guess."

Indian Affairs paid her way to Algonquin College in Ottawa. She took Law and Security. "I was always interested in law, no idea why. No one in my family, not aunts, uncles, no one had been a cop. Maybe because I was the enforcer at home, the strong one."

After graduation, she applied to the Ottawa-Carlton Detention Centre and was accepted as a corrections officer. She found the superintendent would constantly single her out for introductions when big shots were visiting the place; when she asked why, he said, "You're a woman. And a native."

She wasn't sentimental in the least about the prisoners. "We didn't have much in the way of relationships. We were there to guard them, give them their meals, escort them from place to place, since they're not permitted to move freely through the centre, make sure they cleaned their cells, and didn't fight in the day rooms. There were about a thousand inmates, male and female. I did get tired of working there—my first love was to be a police officer."

Math was only a twenty-minute segment of the entrance exam, but her problems kept haunting her, screwing up her chances. She was determined to beat this foe, and worked with flash cards to better her accuracy and speed. When an opening came up in Toronto, she was confident.

"This officer came in, and said if we call your name, you're leaving, going back home; if we don't, you passed, you're staying. He didn't call my name, but I still didn't believe it. So I went up to him and said, 'I passed the math?' And I had!"

SUSAN MCCOY,
TORONTO POLICE SERGEANT

Susan McCoy was an only child growing up in the High Park area of Toronto, where the triplex she lived in backed on to Catfish Pond. Her dad was an electrician, her mom a hairdresser (not a hair stylist).

Susan spent her after-school hours at the beauty parlour, in the company of women. This, as well as the fact that most of her weekends involved visiting her grandparents' dairy farm, left her ill-equipped for relating to children her own age.

She was at McMaster University when she realized that although she was doing well academically, she was a "social nerd." She lived off campus with a couple who rented to students, and she spent most of her time studying. Independent by nature, she hated asking her parents for five or ten dollars to get through the month; she wanted to earn her own money and also to experience some of the world that had seemed to pass her by: different social norms, lifestyles, and experiences.

So Susan took a summer job in a Youth and the Law Program, where students could work in a real police environment. Her assignment was to the Police Museum, then located at 590 Jarvis. She did research work and displays—

it was a world she knew nothing about. Every day, on her way to work, she had to pass the employment office, and the recruiting sergeant kept saying to her: "C'mon in." She ignored him for a long while, then thought, they won't take me anyway, so why don't I just fill in the papers and shut him up? Unexpectedly, she got a call towards the end of her school year, asking if she could start in January.

"I thought I could try it for a year or two. Next January will be my twenty-fifth year."

JAY HOPE, OPP COMMANDER

Jay was born to a middle-class family in Scarborough, just outside Toronto. His dad had immigrated from Barbados and worked on oil rigs for twenty-one years before sending himself to night school to earn a teaching degree, landing a job at Forest Hill Collegiate. His mother also went to night school, after her husband's graduation, and became a business teacher.

There were only two black children in his public school and four in his high school. He describes himself as a kid who was athletic and a bit of a class clown. School wasn't difficult, if and when he applied himself. He remembers a grade-eight teacher telling his parents that he'd never make it to university, and his father saying, in effect, this conversation is not happening, he will go. He was the grade-thirteen valedictorian, and won the Principal's Medal for Citizenship and Academics.

Jay lived in a predominately Italian area, and he had no

real experience of racism that he can remember, until grade seven, when another student called him a "nigger." He remembers feeling shocked, remembers too that he was so debilitated by the slur that tears came to his eyes. His friends wanted him to beat up the guy, but he couldn't do it. He knew the word, knew he was black, but the world he lived in had been so sheltered from all that evil that he himself even used, when picking teams for sports, the old rhyme: "Eenie, meenie, mynie, moe, catch a nigger by the toe," without any awareness of its hateful nature.

He'd always wanted to be either an actor or a cop. He had an uncle, by way of marriage, in the Toronto force, and he was struck by how much autonomy he had. "My uncle and his partner would say "we'll see you for lunch," and they'd drive up in their squad car. They seemed to have a lot of freedom. I wanted that kind of control over my destiny, I wanted to tell people what to do rather than be told."

He signed up immediately on graduation from university. He'd briefly considered the Toronto force, but at the time things were going badly between the black community and the police, over shootings, and the force was being accused of racism. He applied to the Peel Police, got turned down, then was immediately accepted by the OPP.

Jay is an ambitious, take-charge kind of guy; he makes no apologies for this. When he's on the news, he looks like a southern state trooper, really intimidating, with his hat tilted forward, his broad arms folded against his chest.

MARGO BOYD, TORONTO POLICE INSPECTOR

Margo was born in Brantford, Ontario, and raised from the age of seven or eight in North Toronto. After just the barest pause for thought, she describes her family as upper-middle-class and herself as "spoiled." She cites the fact that her parents bought her a horse as proof of that spoiling. Her dad worked in management at a sales company, and her mother was a housewife.

"My mother wouldn't appreciate that description, she wasn't at all a traditional housewife; she didn't bake cookies or anything, and she was involved in social agencies such as Street Haven and the Donwood."

Though neither of her parents had been to university, her mother "is one of the brightest people I know and a voracious reader. We would have real discussions at our house, about politics and current events."

She was taught respect for money, she had a part-time job selling clothes, and she did some modelling. A university education was assumed; she would go, and go she did, attending York and gaining a B.A. in psychology. She was the only one of her friends from Earl Haig Secondary School to go; some married right out of high school, some went to college for their nursing certificates.

It was about 1975—Angie Dickinson had a television show called *Police Woman*—when her dad let her know there were openings on the Toronto force. It seemed there was nothing much else a woman with a B.A. in psychology could do, other than earn $5,000 a year as a salesperson.

"I went down and asked about openings and they told me there was a school crossing guard position, but I asked about being a cop and was told there was a two-year waiting list. I filled out the forms anyway, and six weeks later I got the call to come in for an interview."

Margo is married to Mike Boyd; they met on the force, but she doesn't share his reserve. A born story-teller, she punctuates her tales with infectious laughter.

GLEN BANNEN, ANISHINABEK POLICE SERVICES CHIEF

Glen grew up in Northern Ontario, at Fort William First Nation Reserve, just outside Thunder Bay.

I expect that everyone who talked to me did so out of a variety of motives, but no one was as blatant as Glen, who gave me the phone numbers of government bureaucrats deciding budget allocations, urging me to call and ask about inequities. He has a lot of "hustler" in him, which can make him annoying and likable at the same time.

His father "was close to one hundred percent Indian" and his mother was first-generation Ukrainian. There were about three hundred people on the reserve then (it's grown to between 1,400 and 1,800) and they really loved and accepted his mother, although her mother's father wasn't happy about her marrying an Indian. He'd come to the reserve and raise hell sometimes, but he came around. Having grandchildren helped.

"Dad was a professional alcoholic; he played ball and other sports on the reserve and earned a living shovelling grain out of cars. He was quick, he could do in three or four hours what took other guys twice as long." He remembers they were the first family on the reserve to get indoor toilets and the first to get television.

"I went to Indian day school for grades one to three; it was right across from my house—the one-room model. If I needed to go to the bathroom, I'd run home rather than use the school's outhouse." For grades four through eight, he went to nine different elementary schools in the Catholic system. If a school had more kids than expected, it was easier to transfer the Indian kids than the locals. By the time he reached high school—Selkirk Collegiate and Vocational—he was ready to settle in. He joined the school band and became president of the student council.

"I was very fortunate that the guys I ran with all through high school (there were maybe eight to ten of us) understood what it was like to be seen as different: They were Italians, Japanese, Polish, Ukrainian, and Indians. If someone was giving the Italian guy grief, the rest of us would deal with the troublemaker. It was a warm, loving group of people who suffered through the same dysfunctional crap; all are now good members of AA. Some work in construction, some are doctors and lawyers."

He met his future wife in grade nine. She was also in the school band, but "She was artsy; I was tech."

His Ukrainian grandfather had introduced him to the violin, but he could soon play most of the available instruments. He won Youth of the Year in Arts for his playing. After school was done, while his wife studied forestry at Lakehead University, he held a variety of jobs: plumber, carpenter, taxi driver. Then he heard that Fort William was looking for "a reserve copper," and he applied.

Appendix
Policing in Canada

In 1999, according to Statistics Canada, there were about 55,000 public police. In addition, over 70,000 specialized private police provided security as employees or on a for-hire basis.

JURISDICTIONS

Public policing is provided by the federal, provincial, and some municipal governments. Governments in Canada can also authorize other, limited policing, such as Harbour Police, Military Police, and Railway Police.

The Royal Canadian Mounted Police (RCMP), the largest single police force in Canada, is our country's federal agency. In addition to performing their musical ride and guarding embassies and other national buildings, the RCMP investigates organized crime, narcotics, and commercial fraud. They administer crime detection laboratories, the

Canadian Police Information Centre (CPIC), and colleges in Regina and Ottawa. They also run a fleet of patrol boats and an aviation unit, and special native constables work under their direction. The RCMP's commissioner is appointed by the governor-in-council.

Two provincial governments, Ontario and Quebec, have their own police forces. All other provinces, the territories, and numerous municipalities hire the RCMP on contract. (The Royal Newfoundland Constabulary provides policing services in several of that province's municipalities.)

Most of Canada's large municipalities have their own police forces, often called Police Services.

POWERS AND AUTHORITY

The traditional powers of police—crime prevention and detection, apprehension of offenders, protection of life and property, and maintenance of order—have increased in recent years. Monitoring deviant actions, surveillance, and crowd control are among these new duties, along with such controversial jobs as the selective enforcement of pornography violations. Although federal laws—especially the Criminal Code—limit some police powers, the provinces have primary responsibility, through Police Acts. All public police are responsible to an elected civil authority. However, in performing their duties, police have considerable discretionary power.

BOARDS AND COMMISSIONS

To avoid (at least the appearance of) political interference, most jurisdictions appoint boards or commissions.

The Toronto Police Services Board's seven members include the mayor (or designate), two city councillors, an appointee of the city's Council, and three appointees of the provincial government. The Police Services Act sets out the Board's mandate. Broadly speaking, the Board oversees the provision of police services in the city—management and policy—but it does not direct the police chief in daily or other operational matters.

The Ontario Civilian Commission on Police Services exercises certain supervisory and regulatory powers over all the province's municipal Police Services and Boards. The Commission oversees maintenance of standards by police forces and Boards, conducts investigations into police matters and law enforcement, and investigates complaints—and holds hearings about—police services or conduct. All commission members are appointed by orders-in-council.

Most municipal police forces are governed by their municipal councils or their committees.

ASSOCIATIONS AND UNIONS

Almost all large police forces in Canada have some form of employee group, which are called or act as a union. The major exception is the RCMP. In addition, there are a number of police associations that exist only to provide information sharing, networking, and education to their members.

TRAINING

Qualifications for entrants vary among jurisdictions, and no standard training exists for Canadian police. The RCMP offers a twenty-two-week course in Regina; the Maritimes, Quebec, Ontario, and British Columbia have regional training centres, which provide basic training that lasts an average of twelve weeks; and various centres offer specialized courses.

For example, when recruits are accepted into the Ontario Provincial Police (OPP), they attend the Provincial Police Academy in Orillia for a one-week introductory session, then complete a twelve-week diploma course at the Ontario Police College in Aylmer (a requirement of all police in Ontario), and conclude training with a three-week session in Orillia. At that point, they become constables and begin their duties.

Toronto's C.O. Bick College provides that city's police with an equivalent to the OPP's Academy courses in Orillia. Police can take advanced courses or specialized training at such centres as the OPP Academy, the RCMP's Canadian Police College in Ottawa, and the FBI Academy in Virginia, U.S.A. Academic studies can be pursued through community colleges and universities.